LOVE'S LONG LINE

21ST CENTURY ESSAYS

David Lazar and Patrick Madden, Series Editors

LOVE'S LONG LINE

Sophfronia Scott

MAD CREEK BOOKS, AN IMPRINT OF
THE OHIO STATE UNIVERSITY PRESS
COLUMBUS

Library of Congress Cataloging-in-Publication Data
Names: Scott, Sophfronia, author.
Title: Love's long line / Sophfronia Scott.
Other titles: 21st century essays.
Description: Columbus : Mad Creek Books, an imprint of The Ohio
    State University Press, [2018] | Series: 21st century essays | Includes
    bibliographical references.
Identifiers: LCCN 2017043667 | ISBN 9780814254639 (pbk. ; alk. paper) |
    ISBN 0814254632 (pbk. ; alk. paper)
Subjects: LCSH: Scott, Sophfronia. | Grief. | Faith. | Motherhood. | Forgiveness.
    | Families.
Classification: LCC PS3619.C684 Z46 2018 | DDC 814/.6 [B]—dc23
LC record available at https://lccn.loc.gov/2017043667

Cover design by Nathan Putens
Text design by Juliet Williams
Type set in Adobe Sabon and ITC Franklin Gothic

For Darryl

. . . you reel out love's long line alone, stripped like a live wire loosing its sparks to a cloud, like a live wire loosed in space to longing and grief everlasting.

—Annie Dillard, *Holy the Firm*

CONTENTS

PART FOUR · THE REALM OF SPIRIT BARE

CODA

ACKNOWLEDGMENTS

"A Boy's Grief" appeared in *Hotel Amerika*.

"Why I Didn't Go to the Firehouse" appeared in *The Timberline Review*.

"For Roxane Gay: Notes from a Forgiving Heart" appeared in the *Ruminate Magazine* blog.

"Calling Me By My Name" appeared in *Killens Review of Arts & Letters*.

"White Shirts" appeared in *Numéro Cinq*.

"Tain in the Rain" appeared in *The Newtowner*.

"The Payoff Letter" appeared in *Sleet Magazine*.

"Why I Must Dance Like Tony Manero" appeared in *Ruminate Magazine*.

"Spiritual Journey Mile Marker: Rob Bell, NYC" appeared in the *Ruminate Magazine* blog.

"Opening to Love" appeared in the *Ruminate Magazine* blog as "The Definition of an Open Heart."

"Of Flesh and Spirit" appeared in *Awst Press*.

"A Faith of Pure Imagination" appeared in *Sleet Magazine*.

"Honoring Autumn: A Dervish Essay" appeared in *Barnstorm Literary Journal*.

In my previous writing life I worked as a newsmagazine journalist, and what I learned at those fine publications was all I knew about nonfiction. So when I entered the Vermont College of Fine Arts (VCFA) to study fiction and my friend the writer Robert Vivian suggested I learn creative nonfiction as well, I had a good and hearty laugh. *What is creative nonfiction?* It sounded like something that would have gotten me fired at my old job! But our conversations on the subject helped me to see myself not as a fiction writer or an essay writer or a poet but as a writer, period. And the more avenues I have of transforming what I want to say into the written word, the better. I embarked on the journey of creative nonfiction and the result, so far, is this book. None of these essays would exist if my friend had not nudged me to write in this genre. He also inspired me, with his mastery of dervish essays, to experiment with the form and write "Honoring Autumn." I thank him with an abundance of appreciation.

I am deeply grateful for Tain, who has never flinched at having a Mama who sometimes writes about him. He is a patient and loving subject.

I also send huge thanks and a bounty of gratitude to:

David Lazar and Patrick Madden for teaching me about the centuries-old banquet that is essay writing, and showing me I have a seat at the table.

Kristen Elias Rowley and the fantastic team at The Ohio State University Press and Mad Creek Books for creating a beautiful book and giving it a home.

My VCFA advisors Lawrence Sutin, Patrick Madden, and Bret Lott, whose guidance has been invaluable.

The glorious cloud of writers who have read and supported my essay writing: Richard Bausch, Charles Baxter, Liz Blood, Mathieu Cailler, Breena Clarke, Dede Cummings, Renee D'Aoust, Matthew Dickman, Douglas Glover, Christina Haag, Sonya Huber, Richard Jackson, Richard Jarrette, Peter Orner, William Pierce, Donald Quist, Martha Southgate, Michelle Webster-Hein, and Peter Wright.

Brianna Van Dyke and Renee Long for providing a space at *Ruminate* where I can explore ideas.

Paul Matthew Carr for designing my author website, where I can explore even more.

The Wheelers—David, Fran, Nate, Ben, and Matty with much love.

My mother and my siblings because I know I write of hard things.

David Hicks for being the best writing buddy in the world.

Carl Nagin, who told me many, many years ago that I could be a writer. He unknowingly changed my life.

Brettne Bloom, my agent, and Heather Jackson, my first book editor, for putting me on the path.

My writing life is blessed because it is filled with so many caring and loving people. I hope that love radiates from these pages.

PART ONE

SPARKS AND LIVE WIRES

A BOY'S GRIEF

---

*I*n the weeks following the shootings at my son's school, the children of Sandy Hook Elementary did not play outside. That January they started classes in an old middle school building the next town over. "Mothballed," officials had called it, forsaken for a new facility, constructed next door, several years earlier. To accommodate the Sandy Hook children the old building needed to be brought up to code. And, since it had been a school for older students, it had no playground. The work on a new playground began despite the cold. Tain, then eight and a third grader, was excited by the prospect of a fresh slide and untouched swings. He would come home and report on the progress he viewed in glimpses from the school bus or classroom windows. But I got the sense that no one was in a hurry to have the children outside. Police officers stood vigilant at the school's entrance and also at the driveway near the road. The prying eyes of the media, so hot in the days after the shootings they threatened to melt every ounce of patience and resolve the town had left, still roamed. As for the children—many were sensitive to loud noises, and some were afraid to go upstairs in their own homes.

After a few weeks Tain grew tired of the indoor recesses, and one day at home he told me he wanted to play outside. I was surprised—he didn't ask me or his father to go out with him, and I knew he didn't particularly like playing outside alone in the cold. But I was glad he wanted to go. I helped him bundle up in his coat and boots. I pulled a knit cap down over his thick black curls and drew a stick of balm over his pink lips. Then he went out into the yard. I took my laptop into the family room where I could keep an eye on him through the windows while I worked. At first he walked around in the yard, stomping lightly as though he were testing the frozen ground beneath his feet. He went over to the swing set and slid down the slide and sat on one of the blue plastic swings. I focused on my computer screen and wrote a few lines. When I looked up again Tain was in the woods, climbing the stony slope behind our house. I knew where he was going—to the plateau where a huge fallen tree served as both bridge and fort. In the summer the leaves of the trees close off this space from the view of the house and it becomes a giant, adventure-ready playroom. I usually sit on the deck and monitor Tain and his friends by listening. On that cold day I moved my laptop to the kitchen table and cracked open the sliding glass doors off the deck just enough so I could hear him. After awhile Tain's voice did come floating through the screen door. He was kind of singing, kind of talking, and I smiled, thinking he was talking to himself. He seemed to be telling a story from the Club Penguin game he often played on our kitchen computer. But who was he telling it to? Then I realized—maybe he wasn't really alone.

This was how he had played with his friend Ben. Ben was among the young victims of the shooting, his classroom just a few hundred feet down the hall from Tain's. Was Tain in search of his friend in their special place in the woods? Could he feel Ben's presence as he walked over the smooth trunk of the fallen tree? I felt a strange comfort in the possibility. I knew he was grieving and if he could connect in some way with a feeling of Ben then that would tell me he was working his own process. Only Tain knew and knows the depth of his loss and the shock of realizing a child even younger than himself can die. He has few words for the magnitude of what's happened, and perhaps it is adult folly to think I can accurately describe a void where love once stood. But I can ponder and I can hope. If he was walking through the soft shadows of his grief, even if accompanied by a kind of ghost, I knew he would have the best chance of emerging on the other side. C. S. Lewis, writing after the death of his wife Joy in *A Grief Observed,* wondered why he had no dreams of her during his deepest grief. It was only after the edge had worn off and he felt a little better that she appeared in a dream. I felt whether or not Ben appeared to Tain—and how he appeared—would determine the way in which Tain walked through the world, whether he could live in faith and not fear. So I was heartened by the sound of Tain chattering in the woods.

I know it may seem strange to entertain this realm of possibility, to want my child to consort with beings beyond the veil. But I grew up in a family where echoes of the dead provided a soundtrack to which my father seemed especially attuned. When I was about eight years old my father's fraternal twin, Virgil, became gravely ill. We made the trek from Lorain, Ohio, to St. Louis, my first car trip, so Daddy could visit him in the hospital. Uncle Virgil died after we returned home. I remember standing behind my mother when she went into their bedroom that day to give Daddy the sad news. The curtains were closed, but sunlight in tiny straws illuminated a fraction of the room. He was sitting on the side of the bed and my mother told him Virgil had died. Daddy said, "I know. My mama already came in here and told me Virgil passed." I knew his mother had died when he was very young so I looked carefully around me. The tiny blue room was so small—the bed and two dresser drawers took up the whole space. My father, if he wanted to, could reach out and almost touch the doorless closet in front of him. My mother and I filled the area in front of the doorway. Was there enough room for his mother to be present still? Could I reach out and feel her in the air? A part of me wanted to be afraid but another part of me wasn't because Daddy wasn't. He seemed to take it as a matter of fact that the dead appeared this way. And Daddy wasn't the kind of man you questioned, especially if you were a child who knew better than to open your mouth at such a time. But there was a certainty in his slumped shoulders and the way he held his calloused hands clasped in front of him. She had been there because he said so.

Sixteen years later on the night of the January day Daddy died my sister Theodora said she awoke to see him out in our front yard near her bedroom window of the tiny pink-shingled house we grew up in. Her dog, a small terrier, was outside barking. Daddy was wearing the black and red plaid hunter's jacket he used to wear when we were younger and he seemed to be surveying the house and yard. Daddy told Theo to take the dog in because he was tired of the noise. He also reminded her to take down the Christmas lights still decorating the house and trees. She responded as we have always done. "Yes, sir."

A friend asked if my town is now filled with ghosts—whether one can sense these children, for instance, playing on the banks of the Pootatuck River that runs through the center of Sandy Hook or sledding down the hills of Treadwell Park where trees have been planted to honor them and the adults who died with them that day. But it doesn't work like that, or at least I don't think it does. It seems to me unknown ghosts are rarely spotted. They only appear when you have business with them. You can only conjure a presence you know as well as your own because ghosts are echoes of ourselves, traces of unfinished business. Some vital part of us remains connected to departed souls. That part cries out for them and this is how they respond—gently, peripherally, in way just outside of our consciousness. Tain does have a great love for and unfinished business with Ben.

Ben lived with his older brother Nate and his parents David and Francine. My husband Darryl and I knew David first and then, when he started dating her, Francine. We were friends in New York City in that way where your friends are your family. Our family was a tight core of musicians, actors, and writers. We spent Thanksgiving together and eventually hosted David and Francine's engagement party. I recall babysitting Nate, then three months old, holding him in my arms in their Queens apartment while watching the first stages of that year's Tour de France.

Somewhere there's a photo of me, taken three years later, my arms filled with a newborn baby Ben.

Darryl and I left New York six months after Tain was born and settled in Sandy Hook, Connecticut, because it was quiet and a reasonable commute to his teaching job, then in Stamford. And we liked the woods behind the house, certain it would become a playground someday for Tain. A few years later David and Francine joined us, moving into a house just five minutes away. When we tell the story of their move I joke that they were stalking us. David says we were simply their advance team. Truth be told, I was delighted to have friends so close and that Nate, Ben, and Tain could grow up together. The boys got along so well. Tain, when he was about five, talked about having a band with Nate and Ben, and wondered how soon they could go on gigs. We have video of them, Nate at the piano and Tain and Ben banging away on percussive instruments. You can see how eager Ben is to follow Tain around the room and take his cues.

When Tain and I were baptized at Trinity Episcopal Church in November 2011 we chose Francine as his godmother. It didn't take long for Tain to happily co-opt the whole family. He called Nate and Ben his godbrothers; Francine's parents became his god-grandparents. Though he was closer in age to Nate (he was a year younger than Nate), as a playmate he was closer to Ben. Nate and Ben would come over and Nate would only want to sit indoors and read or sometimes join the boys at the kitchen computer if they were playing a game he liked. But Tain and Ben loved to be outside, jumping in piles of leaves or rambling through the woods. A brief essay Tain wrote for his teacher just weeks before the shootings was called "Hike with Ben" and described one of their outings. He called Ben "a good climber" and noted how Ben "said things like dum dum want gum gum!" The last line of the piece: "This was a time that Ben and I would never forget!"

Tain attended a private school for kindergarten, first, and second grades. Then in the spring of 2012, seemingly out of nowhere, he said, "I want to try Sandy Hook School. I want to go to school with Nate and Ben." This was nine months before the tragedy. Parents don't change schools on a child's whim, but requests like this from Tain are rare. When they come up, I listen. First we waited to see if he would repeat his request and he did. I checked in several times with his teachers to make sure nothing was making him unhappy where he was. Finally I took him to tour the school—easily done because it was only minutes from our home. There had been several changes at Sandy Hook Elementary, including the principal, since Darryl and I had gone to the kindergarten orientation years before. I liked the way this principal, Dawn Hochsprung, walked the halls with Tain and addressed his questions about lunch and recess. She showed him the ducks outside that made the schoolyard their home. I could tell he liked her right away too by the way he skipped along beside her.

That autumn, after his first day of school, Tain bounded off the bus and joyfully announced, "I saw Ben!"

A few weeks later Tain told me about this photo:

Ben and Tain
September 2012

Some would say it's not even a real photograph. It's a cheap computer image spit out by a machine at a pizza chain restaurant.

Tain came home from Ben's sixth birthday party and told me how he and Ben took a great picture together in the photo booth.

"That's wonderful," I said. "Let's see it."

"Well," Tain held up his empty palms and smiled. "Ben really liked it so I said he could have it."

I could tell from his wide toothy grin he was proud of his "big boy" gesture. I was too and I hugged him.

"Ben is so lucky to have a friend like you."

In my calendar for December 14, 2012, I'd blocked off all of the hours after school and into the evening with the label "Babysit Nate and Ben." David and Francine were planning to enjoy a rare evening out. The night before I stood in front of the pantry in my kitchen thinking about what I would feed the boys. Both Nate and Ben have nut allergies. And Ben was always asking me for snacks—"O's" or Cheerios when he was younger, then later cheese sticks and chocolate milk. He would ask even when Fran said he'd just eaten.

To my left Tain sat at our kitchen computer planning the games, including Animal Jam, he and his godbrothers would play, and the new levels on Club Penguin he wanted to show them. I thought about how one moment they would be arguing over whose turn was next and in the next moment be laughing themselves silly because they were little boys like that.

I mention these plans because that's where Tain's head was when Darryl brought him home from the firehouse where the Sandy Hook children had waited to be reunited with family in the aftermath of the shootings. He said he was cold and asked for hot chocolate.

"We didn't get to take our coats."

"I know." I hugged him and rubbed his back. "We'll get you warmed up. You can stand in front of the fireplace and I'll make you some hot chocolate."

"When are Nate and Ben coming over?"

"I don't know." I looked at Darryl and then at my phone in my hand. Texts from Fran and then our pastor told me Nate was fine but Ben was unaccounted for. The last I heard David was checking the local hospitals to see if he had been taken to one.

"Tain, do you know what happened at your school today?"

He nodded. "Robbers broke into the school," he said. "The Army came to help stop them."

"That's almost right. A lot of people came to help. There were lots of people there, right?"

He nodded again.

"But it was only one person—a man who came into the school with a gun. Right now we don't know everything that's happened, but a lot of people are hurt."

His voice dropped to a whisper. "I heard one of the kids say the principal died."

I squeezed Tain's arm. "Yes, that's right. She died."

Tain shook his head. "Why did the man do that?"

"We don't know Tain. Like I said, everyone is still trying to figure it out."

"But Nate and Ben are still coming over?"

"I don't know. Let's get you some hot chocolate and we'll wait and see, okay?"

"Okay."

Night fell. That's when the text from my pastor arrived.

No survivors.

I took the phone into the kitchen and showed it to Darryl. Tain, sitting at the computer, asked his question again.

"When are Nate and Ben coming over?"

I sighed and looked at Darryl. He stood with his arms crossed, his face knotted with sadness. "Tain, come here," I said.

I took his hand and held it in both of mine.

"Ben didn't come home from school."

"How come?"

"Because he got hurt really badly, Tain. He was hurt and they couldn't save him and he died."

Tain's face dissolved. His big eyes melted into thin lines and his mouth opened in an awful slow motion. At first nothing came out—only a horrible frozen silence like his body couldn't figure out how to take in enough breath for the cry it wanted to form.

When the sound finally emerged it rose from deep within his chest, a solid wail harsh and raw. His tears flowed hot and fast.

"I don't want Ben to be dead!" He sobbed.

I felt my heart crumbling into brittle, futile pieces. I wanted to take it all back, to say none of it was true, to retrieve the cord of grief I saw unraveling and sparking wildly, uncontrollably into the air around us. But I couldn't do that. No one can do that. Life only moves forward.

I put my arms around Tain and held him tightly. "I know, I know. We're all going to be crying for a long time. We're all going to be sad for a really long time."

Eventually I put my hands on his face and looked into his eyes. "Tain, you're going to have to be really strong because you have to help Nate. Nate's going to miss Ben so much and you have to be there for him. I'm going to call their house now and I'm going to go over there in a bit. You don't have to go, but you think about it. If you feel you can go, you can come with me."

I went into my office and called to make sure David and Francine were at home. I can't remember who I spoke to, but I remember asking if it was okay for me to bring Tain and they had said yes.

When I returned to the kitchen Tain had wiped his face and was nodding at me.

"I want to help Nate."

"Okay, bud. That's great. And you will. We all will."

Tain didn't get to help Nate right away. Before I left for their house I received another message that Fran couldn't bear to see Tain.

Then noise—days upon days of noise. The first of it I can barely remember because it hurts too much to do so. I recall the fresh screams of grief and holding Fran so tightly because I could feel the world coming apart around us and the only thing that seemed real were the people solemnly crying with us. The phone in our home and theirs began to ring incessantly—family, friends, and media, all calling.

A day or two later when I was able to bring Tain to the house he spent most of the time in the playroom, sometimes with Nate and sometimes with the children of family and friends. At one point he used a bunch of Legos to spell out "Ben" on the carpet. He asked me to take a picture of him with this creation.

Ben's family received visitors in our church sanctuary the day before the funeral. The parishioners lovingly pitched in and filled the space with what Ben loved—lighthouses and stuffed animals and photographs of friends and family. In the chapel a monitor showed, in a running loop, pictures of Ben with his friends. I walked through the display with Tain. Every so often he'd say, "Ben would have loved that."

When we got to the photo montage Tain stood in front of the monitor for a long time. He watched the images floating past, viewing the completed loop at least three times. Finally he asked, "Why am I in only one picture?"

He was right. Tain was in one photo with Ben and a few other boys. I'd never seen it before and it looked like it was from someone's birthday party.

"I don't know. You know Papa and I sent in lots of pictures for this. Maybe they didn't get them."

We watched the pictures a little longer. Tain remained silent.

The next morning Darryl left for the funeral early because he was singing in the choir and had to rehearse. We had guests in the house so I had them on my mind on top of getting Tain and myself ready. Fortunately Tain's dress pants still fit him. I put him in a white shirt and a vest. We stood in front of the mirror, Tain clutching a new sandy brown stuffed dog friends had sent for him. I said what I usually say when he's dressed for school: "You look good, bud!"

He was quiet. Then this: "I want to wear pictures of Ben."

"Well, remember we're all wearing pictures of Ben."

I showed him the square badges a friend had made so we could tell who was family and to make sure we were all seated together in what would be a packed church.

"No," Tain said. "I want pictures of me and Ben."

"Okay," I said slowly. Time was getting short. I was responsible for driving a van of family members to the church. But I knew this was a request that had to be answered.

I went to the kitchen computer and found some of the sorted photos Darryl and I had put aside for the wake. I printed up two photos, both from the same day, of Tain and Ben playing in a pile of leaves in our yard. I carefully cut them into squares and fastened them with tape and paper clips to Tain's vest.

"Is that good?"

He looked down at the pictures and nodded and smiled.

At the church whenever anyone asked Tain about the pictures on his clothes he talked about Ben who was his godbrother and how much fun they had playing in the leaves. I was glad to see how Tain felt connected to Ben. In the months to come he surprises me by how quick he is to have such conversations, to want to talk about Ben. When we meet strangers and they find out where we're from, they ask the inevitable questions. I deliver a simple answer that I hope will end the conversation quickly: "Yes, close friends of ours lost their child." But Tain will interject pointedly: "Mama, he wasn't just a friend. He was my *godbrother.*" He held and still holds his grief strong, but lightly, as though he were holding his friend's little hand.

We have two mementos from that day. One is Tain's copy of the funeral program, his name written on the front because he wanted to make sure no one took it by mistake. Inside, in the blank spaces labeled "Children's Art Pages," he drew a large striped lighthouse. Above the lighthouse he drew Ben atop what looks like a cloud or an airplane. I eventually realized this was Tain's rendition of the picture of Ben on the cover of the program.

The other memento is a tall glass candle illustrated with this same picture of Ben superimposed over a Thomas Kinkade painting of tranquil seas. Tain placed it on the table by his bed and it's still there today. The photo booth picture of Ben and Tain from Ben's last birthday party is in our home now too, framed and sitting atop the chest of drawers in Tain's room. Francine, knowing Tain would want to have the picture, gave it to him. For the longest time I would be putting away his T-shirts and sweaters, and after closing the drawers, look up to see the boys' grinning faces and feel a thud in my heart. I am bewildered the picture is there, still shocked at how it's now in Tain's possession.

To be honest, I didn't take Tain to any of the counselors or resiliency sessions made available to the families of our town. I thumbed through the many grief books donated to our local library but none of them connected for me. The one I brought home for Tain, a journal in which a child could paste pictures and write about their lost loved one, failed to pique his interest. I know many parents will think that odd, but I can only explain I sensed aspects of Tain's journey would have to be uniquely his own, perhaps because it involved faith. He already had people all around him, myself included, who could talk to him about God and His presence in all of this. But for him to truly believe, to feel hope and comfort and be upheld in his faith, I knew Tain had to feel it himself. To a certain extent, all I could do was listen. I dusted the Ben candle and the Chuck E. Cheese photograph when I cleaned Tain's room. I waited.

Not long after the day Tain asked to play outside, I was putting him to bed and I asked how he was doing, how he was feeling about Ben. I wasn't sure if this was the right thing to ask and I didn't know what he would say. But he looked at me, his large brown eyes wide with wonder.

"Mama, I just have the feeling I'm going to see Ben again. He's going to come down from Heaven and he's going to be here with all of us."

Each week in our church we recite the Nicene Creed. The last line of it says, "We look for the resurrection of the dead, and the life of the world to come."

Tain's words tell me he's internalized this, perhaps even better than most adults who believe the same. He knows it in a deeper way than I can ever comprehend. This knowing might even be strengthened because he already sensed Ben's presence in the woods. I hope and pray he receives some kind of affirmation to help him maintain his belief.

"Yes," I told him. "I think you're right."

As Tain, now 11, approaches the tween years I am wary, more now than before. He comes home talking about what kids say on the bus. The children are older now, more cynical. They like to repeat, with precious little understanding, what they've heard from adults. The topic of death comes up often.

Recently Tain and I were having dinner in a sushi restaurant in New York City. He told me about yet another conversation the kids had on his bus about what happens after you die.

"They say there's nothing afterwards," he said and he shrugged. "Everything just goes black." He stabbed at a piece of California roll with his chopsticks.

"Does that sound right to you?" I asked.

He shrugged again. "I don't think so."

I handed him a napkin and took a sip from my cup of green tea. "You know, there are a lot of stories of people who died but a doctor or a paramedic was able to resuscitate them," I said. "None of them said anything about everything going to black. In fact, it was just the opposite. They talked about seeing a bright light and having the feeling of leaving their bodies and being able to see everyone as they floated above them."

"Is that how they can come to you and make you have visions and dreams?"

I was using my chopsticks to mix a dab of wasabi into the shallow dish of soy sauce and I was about to say, "Yes, that's right." But something made me stop and look at Tain. He had put his chopsticks down; his hands were folded in his lap. I could see the depth of his question sitting in the slight furrow of his brow.

Finally I asked, "Who have you seen?"

He looked at me and said the name with a calm but heavy certainty.

"Ben."

"Where were you? What did he say?"

"We weren't really anywhere, we were just kind of floating in space. It was like he's been away on vacation and he was asking me how things are since he left. I told him he has a new baby brother."

"Did you get to ask him anything?"

"I asked him how it was where he is. He said it's really nice and he got to meet God and Jesus." Tain grew quiet. When he spoke again I could hear tears in his throat.

"I don't like to talk about it," he said. "It makes me very sad."

"How come?"

"I just miss Ben a lot."

His tears flowed fully then. I went to his side of the table and held him. I told him we all missed Ben, but how wonderful that Ben came to him, that he got to visit with his friend.

"And really, you answered your own question, didn't you? It doesn't all go to black. I think you knew that before. You really know it now."

He nodded.

"That's really amazing, Tain."

He nodded again and wiped his eyes. "Yeah. It's really good."

I'm hoping Tain will always have the awareness to ask questions and to see the answers when they come to him. I'm hoping he'll remember that even in darkness he can find the light, and in the light there is love and familiar faces. I'm hoping this knowledge will buoy him as he journeys onward, even when his travels take him over rough seas full of tears.

I haven't said so to anyone, but now I feel Ben's presence too. He is next to me each time I open the pantry doors in my kitchen. He is asking me for cheese sticks. He is asking me for chocolate milk. I think about whether I have food he likes to eat in the house. I am still waiting to feed this ghost. I want to feed him. I want to thank him for helping Tain.

WHY I DIDN'T GO TO
THE FIREHOUSE

The firehouse is the Sandy Hook Volunteer Fire and Rescue station and it serves my neighborhood here in Newtown, Connecticut. Yes, that Sandy Hook. And yes to the question that I tend to get next: my son Tain did go to school at Sandy Hook Elementary and he was present in his third grade classroom on the morning of December 14, 2012, when a gunman entered the school and took the lives of 26 adults and children including one of Tain's dearest friends, a first grader named Ben. The firehouse is just down the road, perhaps only a few hundred yards from the location of the school. Dickinson Drive is the name of the street and that's appropriate because it is more like a long driveway than a road, leading only to the small parking lot in front of the school. The firehouse is constructed of red brick and the doors of the bays housing the fire trucks are wide and white. Each year after Thanksgiving my family and I visit the firehouse and choose a tall bushy evergreen from the inventory of Christmas trees the firemen sell as a fundraiser. We pay more than if we shopped elsewhere because we want to support this essential but all-volunteer service. The only other time I'd been in the fire-house was probably for a field trip when Tain was in preschool.

Not long after the news of the shootings broke the *New York Times* published a story that reported:

> *Survivors gathered at the Sandy Hook Volunteer Fire and Rescue station house, just down the street. Parents heard—on the radio, or on television, or via text messages or calls from an automated, emergency service phone tree—and came running.*

I didn't.

I didn't come running.

I could have. The school is not far from my home and that morning I was even closer, at a nearby auto repair shop. But instead of driving out of the shop's parking lot, turning right onto Berkshire Road, and speeding my way to Tain's school I turned left and went home. Why? And I think "Why?" is the more polite question. I get asked about this a lot, from family, friends, strangers. They ask, "What did you do when you found out?" I tell them I went home. Then there's a look on the face in front of me—blank like a sheet of new paper—and when I see that look it seems to me the question they really want to ask is, "How could you do that?" Even if they don't ask it outright, I know the question is there.

Different people handle things differently—we all know that, right? But when I see that look I know the person is running an emotional inventory that could place me somewhere from being a monk to a monster. The space within that range is broad but I think it's the extremes that fascinate the most. On the one end, to not go racing to the firehouse might seem to them faithful and stoic—picture me meditating in front of the Buddha I keep in my office at home—or on the other end, the reaction could seem cold and unfeeling, more nihilistic or existential I suppose. *What kind of mother are you?* In that realm I'm a few wire hangers shy of Joan Crawford in *Mommie Dearest*. But no matter where I fall in someone's spectrum I can see why my response or non-reaction would be confusing, curious, challenging to my listener. Can I say it feels the same for me? It's so hard to explain.

Tell me you would have gone. Tell me how if it had been your son in that school you would have raced right over there like all those parents on television. I will nod and perhaps even mumble something like, "Yes, well . . ." and not finish the sentence. Because your saying that won't get us any closer to the answer to your question. Or maybe that's the point. It's not really about what I did or didn't do. It's about you putting yourself in the picture. People constantly use that phrase, "I can't imagine . . ." and yet I find they do a wonderful job of doing just that. Even if they don't vocalize it I know they are playing out the possibilities.

But their calculations wouldn't include the variable of time. Specifically I mean everything I thought and did in the days, months, and years leading up to that morning. My response after hearing the news wasn't the reaction of a moment. The decisions I made in those early minutes were actually years in the making and informed by seemingly unconnected events. How do you talk about that in the course of a casual conversation?

The repetition of the question, however, tells me something or someone wants an answer. It may even be something deep within myself demanding accountability or acknowledgment. I won't know until I begin so I will attempt a response, but I'm wary—the words I lay out here may be only breadcrumbs that get devoured by greedy ravens—gone that quickly. Or they may stay and pave a path or even a bridge to something more. I have no idea what will happen but I sense this is important and worth the risk. I will try. I'm going to revisit that morning as best I can, with a few prompts such as emails and texts aiding my memory but really, I'm not dependent on them. Such moments are as simple, fierce, and bracing as a cold clear winter day. There's not much you can do to smudge it up. There is only what is.

This essay is about a window of time, a space of approximately two hours, in which I didn't know if my son was safe.

Let's start with the morning, or rather the glow of the morning—pale yellow December light, painted on by a well-worn brush. I had watched that glow develop from the early hours because at the time I was a substitute school bus driver, reporting for work often before 5:30 a.m. with Tain in tow. The dispatcher would hand me a route for a driver who'd called in sick and Tain would ride the bus with me, picking up and delivering first the high school and middle school students, then the intermediate school children. Then, if I wasn't driving a Sandy Hook route, I'd use my break to find a bus that was heading to his elementary school and put him on it before I went on to one of the other three K–5 schools in the Newtown district. I didn't drive to Sandy Hook that morning.

After 9 a.m. I was done and I remember feeling that deep-breath kind of relaxation of work being done for the moment, of having my time be my own again for a little while. I left the bus terminal in my minivan, on my way to Tain's school. Why? I wanted to take a check into the office to refill Tain's lunch money card, which was how the children paid for their meals in the cafeteria. I could have mailed this in or done it online but since my family was still new to Sandy Hook School (Tain had gone to a private school the previous three years) I liked taking such opportunities to visit in person—it was my way of getting more familiar with the principal, Dawn Hochsprung, and the rest of the office staff. I also wanted them to know me. Whenever I went in it seemed Dawn would come right out of her office to see who was there. She'd smile and ask about Tain. She was one of the reasons my husband Darryl and I agreed to make the switch to send Tain to Sandy Hook after Tain expressed an interest in going to school with his friends, including Ben and Nate, Ben's older brother. When we first visited the school I liked how she walked down the hall with Tain, listening carefully to his questions and making him feel as though it were already his school.

So I was on my way there when I remembered the cigarette lighter in the van wasn't working. Darryl had asked me to have it looked at because the next day he had to drive the van to some out-of-town event for the school where he taught seventh and eighth grade band. He needed the GPS, which has to be plugged in to the cigarette lighter. I didn't know how long a fix would take and I was due back to the bus terminal in the afternoon so I decided to stop at the auto repair shop before going to the school.

I think about that particular decision a lot. I still remember the way the thought seemed to float in and settle upon me like a warm blanket—that soft and that obvious. My daddy used to

have a saying, "My mind came to me . . ." whenever he remembered a forgotten detail or a thought occurred to him. This felt
like that. My mind came to me and told me to get the van fixed
first. I know—and for a long time I didn't tell this to anyone—if I
had gone to Tain's school first I would have been there when the
shootings happened. Maybe a few minutes before, maybe a few
minutes after. Maybe I would have been in the office or the parking lot walking to the door.

At the auto shop a woman I knew from my church, Sherry,
was in the waiting room. I sat with her and chatted. I remember
while she waited for her car she was writing thank you notes to
parishioners who had pledged during the church's recent steward-
ship campaign. How long were we sitting there? Not long, maybe
ten or fifteen minutes. A woman walked in with a confused look
clouding her face. She pointed outside to the air behind her and
said she'd gone to the high school (located across the street from
the shop) to pick up her daughter for a dentist appointment but
couldn't get in. Not even onto the grounds.

Then we heard the sound of sirens slashing cleanly through
the cold winter air. Police cars sped past the auto shop.

They weren't stopping at the high school.

All at once it seemed our cellphones were buzzing, Sherry's,
mine, and the woman's, with automated emails, texts, and voicemail messages from the Newtown School District. It said all of
the schools were in a lockdown position with no one allowed
in or out of the buildings because of a shooting at one of the
schools. The messages didn't say which school. I remember the
first breaking news report flashed on the screen of the television in the waiting room. Reports of a teacher shot in the foot. I
remember thinking how absurd the story sounded. Once upon a
time I had been a journalist so I was too familiar with the ridiculous nature of breaking news—how reporters can spew uncon-
firmed facts to fill the airspace that had been wrestled away from
regularly scheduled programming. Sherry grew pale and I wanted
to turn off the television.

Instead I called the school bus depot—I figured the radio system there had access to the same emergency channels used by the
police and ambulances. They would know something real. My

supervisor answered the phone: "Okay, Sophfronia, stay calm," he said. "The shooting is at Sandy Hook." I said okay, then I thanked him and hung up.

After that I was feeling my way through an unknown forest. Already I sought markers, trail blazes, anything that seemed familiar. I asked the shop owner for my van and I went outside to wait for it. Sherry has small children of her own in one of the other elementary schools. Her last words to me before I left the garage: "I'm sorry."

My phone was still in my hand and I stood in the parking lot looking down the road in the direction of the school. In my mind I was already halfway there. *I'm supposed to be doing something. I'm supposed to be doing something.* I wasn't sure what that something was. I had the odd feeling that I was trying to remember something, like I was trying to push through a thicket of brambles to reach a clearing where I could see and think. But despite this I was clear on the one thing I couldn't and could never seem to do in times of trial—I couldn't pray. I remarked on this to my pastor once and she had said, "That's when you have other people pray for you."

I opened the Contacts app on my phone and found Pastor Kathie's number. The photo illustrating her file in my phone is of her, Tain, and me on the day she baptized the both of us the year before. Tain is wearing a navy blue cardigan over his shirt and striped tie and he's holding a gift from his Sunday school class: a cross decorated with seashells. I touched the "Call" symbol next to Pastor Kathie's number. When I told her what was going on she asked in that calm, measured way of hers what I was going to do.

"I'm going over there," I said.

She gently pointed out that I wouldn't be able to do anything there. Her son Miles, an EMT first responder, was already on the scene; she reminded me of how small the roads are in that part of Sandy Hook, how they were most likely already congested, and we had to give the authorities the time and space to get a handle on whatever was going on. My stomach dropped. This could be worse than anyone expected.

"Okay." I may have even said "You're right" but I'm not sure because at that moment it didn't matter. I knew what I was going to do.

She didn't say directly "Don't go" but it was like she had called me back to my right mind and I remembered. I remembered what it was I was supposed to do and I acted, but not out of what it may seem in this part of my account. I know this looks like an obvious answer for you: I didn't go to the firehouse because my pastor suggested against it. Seems simple enough. But her suggesting to me not to go and my listening to her is like saying I went skydiving and I jumped from the airplane because the guy strapped to my back said I had to—a choice but not really a choice.

To say this would discount the thought and preparation, conscious and unconscious, poured into the foundation that one hopes will hold when a moment of crisis arrives. I've never been skydiving but I know in the training you learn how to pull your own ripcord, monitor altitude, and how to position your body so the fall is stable. But all the training in the world wouldn't account for the "screw you" variable that can show itself at any time and obliterate all that has come before it. This variable feeds on drama, fear, excess energy. It rises in the heat of the moment and whether you're skydiving or being presented with any kind of unwanted option you could easily say, even if it's not in your personality to do so, "Screw this."

Screw that, I'm not jumping.

Screw you, my child is in there. I'm going.

It would have been easy to react that way. I felt the pull of emotion and I could have given in to its undertow and told Pastor Kathie in one moment I wouldn't go to the school while doing just that in the next. But as I said, Pastor Kathie called me back to my right mind. I began to act—not out of obedience or even common sense—I began to act intentionally out of a promise I'd made to Tain and myself in the months before he was born.

Right when I arrived home Darryl called. The principal of the middle school where he teaches, about twenty minutes away, had come into Darryl's classroom, told him the news and said he could go home. He was on his way. I called my oldest brother, Vassie. We said a prayer together and stayed in touch throughout the morning. I turned on the television and heard the reporters spewing casualty numbers that seemed to change every few minutes. I turned it off again. I sat at my computer and sent e-mails to three friends chosen specifically because I trust their spirituality.

There's been some sort of shooting at Tain's school. I'm calm but worried, scared. Place is surrounded by troopers and ambulance people. Roads are packed. Waiting here at home for news. Please, please send prayers. I know Tain must be fine and all will be well.

The words "worried" and "scared" weren't accurate but I think I included them because it's what's expected. I wasn't in a state of worry or fear—I was in a void. No, it's more than that. It was like I was in a void and the void was in me. I was holding this space of waiting and the holding of this space was the fulfillment of my promise to Tain.

How can I explain this? I will tell you another story of waiting on another December morning, nine years before this one. I was pregnant then and, to me, miraculously so. I'd had a miscarriage a couple of years earlier, and when Darryl and I couldn't conceive again, we went through tests and discovered my uterus was scarred shut, a result of the treatment following the miscarriage. My gynecologist referred us to an infertility specialist, Dr. K., on the west side of Manhattan and he performed surgery to remove the scar tissue. After a few weeks of healing I was supposed to start taking hormones and undergo more infertility treatment, scheduled to begin after I'd had a period. Only my period never came. We discovered I was already pregnant.

I loved that time of walking newly pregnant through New York City as the days were getting colder. I liked knowing I harbored my own bit of heat, a tiny ball of sunshine growing within me and waiting to warm its own universe. I lived in a realm of possibility and I remember being acutely conscious of it, of soaking up life and magic all around me—savoring the sugar of a Krispy Kreme donut melting in my mouth, my steps touching down on pavement that seemed gentle beneath my feet. I walked down Columbus Avenue and I saw a dual face, my own mingled with some aura of my unborn child, reflected to me in the smiling faces of strangers who couldn't possibly know I was pregnant. But in that strange law of nature, life attracts life, recognizes itself and feeds there. Every face seemed like a harbinger of grace, of the potential held by the being growing inside me. I felt a strong sense of the whole experience being a gift and I was grateful. I loved being in that golden bubble. It felt like where I was supposed to be. It felt like home.

Then suddenly—*blood*.

A Saturday morning, early December, with the first snowstorm of the season whipping a bitter wind past the windows of our sixth floor apartment. I'd gone to the bathroom and found my underwear wet and heavy with thick red clots. The world shrank—shrank so fast the speed burned my eyes. What was so open and available to me the day before became in an instant only the four walls of that space and the bathroom door closed behind me.

I couldn't figure out what would come next. I didn't dare stand for fear of what I might see in the water underneath me. Yet I wanted to get out of the stained underwear already dripping on the black and white tiles. At some point I know I reached for a towel hanging from the bar across from me. At some point I called out for Darryl to help me. But for the longest time I did nothing. The four walls were shrinking further into a hard dark knot and there was no room in there for Darryl, no room for me to even stand and take a step into the moment where I had to accept something was wrong and I had to move into the murkiness of what that meant and what I had to do.

I remember standing in the kitchen calling Dr. K with Darryl sitting on a stool and staring at a cold cup of coffee on the counter in front of him.

"What did the discharge look like?" the doctor asked.

The question made me recall gradations of color—pinks and magentas—apart from the stark red that initially shocked my eyes.

"Is it still happening?"

"Yes."

"I'll be in the office tomorrow morning. We'll do an ultra-
sound and we'll have a look."

Tomorrow?

Why didn't I argue with him? Why didn't I insist he see me
that day? Because I knew Dr. K. I knew him well enough to know
he didn't humor you or give false hope. He was more likely to say,
"This is what we'll do" or "I want to have a look first and we'll
see." His poker-faced way didn't make for a warm bedside manner but I never minded before. In fact I had pitied him because it
seemed to me he needed to be that way from years of experience
with frenzied, baby-yearning Manhattan women. But as I listened
to him on the phone I realized his demeanor was for mornings
just like this one. If he thought something could be done he would
have told me to go to the hospital. I was losing the pregnancy and
probably had to wait for the miscarriage to finish.

And then—darkness. There's the phrase from Psalm 23 about
walking through the valley of the shadow of death but that morning it felt more like a tube—a dark but translucent tube. I could see
the world going on around me and the tube was close enough that
someone could walk next to me without realizing I was in it. But I
knew I was in it, a tight place of sadness, unable to see to the other
end. Inside the tube I tried to maintain the form and potential of a
child I wouldn't get to know. I wanted this because I wanted something more to mourn than the flow draining from between my legs
and because the sense of joy I'd had was once so tangible.

Outside the tube the rest of the world moved on. Darryl and I
were supposed to attend a wedding that day. I'd been looking forward to it because when my friend Katherine had first introduced
Mike to us I somehow sensed he would be the guy she married. I
was thrilled when they got engaged and excited for the wedding.
But that morning I felt heavy with grief, like all my cells were
filled with it, bursting with it. I sat on the couch and hoped for
a phone call saying the weather had forced Katherine and Mike
to postpone. However, it wasn't the shut-down-the-city kind of
snowstorm. The slushy streets were clogged with slow-moving
traffic but you could still walk around, and the trains were running. When it became obvious there'd be no cancellation and Darryl asked if we were still going, I didn't have it in me to say no.

I put on a tan suit—pants and a long jacket to camouflage my bloated waistline—and I went. There are photos of me from that day and looking at them now I can see I was pale. My smile was a game one. I was managing, just hanging on, but faking it all the same. All I wanted to do was go home and go to bed. The wedding and reception took place at a facility in Chelsea right on the Hudson River. If I didn't have the pictures to remind me I was there I might not have remembered much else. I remember the wall of windows showcasing the snow swirling outside on the pier. I remember the bride's broad smile. I remember how the whole space, vibrant with music and voices, was too loud for me to think about how to let go of all the promise my baby-to-be had contained.

The next day at the doctor's office I lay there in the dark, Darryl next to me while Dr. K moved the sensor around within me. I tried to make sense of the fuzzy, wavy lines, but then I saw it: an amazing, pulsating drop of light, insistent and strong.

"There's your baby," the doctor said. "Normal, six-week growth; heart beating and everything."

Darryl asked some questions and Dr. K. answered them—I think he used the words "implantation bleeding" and "normal" but I wasn't listening. I just kept staring at the image on the screen. I was talking to it, saying to it in my heart where only he and I could hear,

I will never give up on you again.

I had walked through that darkness when I didn't have to; and even worse, I'd unwittingly taken my child with me when I did it. The notion damn near overwhelmed me. I'd chosen to believe in death instead of life, had allowed fear to hijack my hope. I focused on the image of my unborn child and promised him I wouldn't do it again. I realized in that moment I must always believe in this little being's life. I had to believe it for both of us. And I still do. That doesn't mean I exist with a Pollyanna kind of hope, acting like Tain, now gloriously present in the world, will never know illness or will never die—because this will happen to all of us. But I do choose to make a simple choice to believe in the greater possibility of life over death, to believe first that life will find a way. It means that as long as Tain's life is a fact, I will live and breathe the joy of it until I know for certain that it's time for me to do otherwise. I hope I will never know such a time, as the grieving Sandy Hook mothers whose children didn't come home now do. However I will not, through fear and worrying, walk myself through the dark valley before I come to it.

So I live out this promise. On any given day it might look like a constant letting go, of watching my son leap from the nest in ways large and small and believing only in his growing ability to fly. My friend Cornelia recently told me it's like I am holding a space for Tain, a space of infinite possibility made all the more powerful because it is his mother who holds it for him. That sounds right to me.

Your question now may be: couldn't I have done that, hold such a space, while waiting at the firehouse with the other parents? Group energy is a powerful thing. If I had gone to the firehouse and walked into that highly emotional brew I probably would have, out of instinct and compassion, mirrored back the concern in the faces of the people around me. And there would be no way to do that without eventually feeling the fear and concern myself. I know how easy it would have been, surrounded by sirens and cameras and weeping, to fret that Tain was injured or dead. I could have lived his death a thousand times in the span of those few hours.

I didn't.

At 11:05 a.m., I received the text from my friend Fran.

Tain is ok.

I typed back fast, while at the same time wanting to collapse to my knees.

How do you know??

I just saw him with his class.

Thank you!!!!! And Nate and Ben?

I can't find Ben.

Within a few minutes another friend was calling with Tain on the phone.

"Hey bud!" I said. "How are you doing?"

I wanted to send him light through my voice, light that would warm him and help him feel a touch of normal in the maelstrom surrounding him.

"Good!"

He said it like he always does, so that the word is almost two syllables with the second syllable toning up like a bounced ball.

I listened for signs of tremors or tears in his voice but I heard none. The one word "good" sounded so like him that I didn't question him about what was happening. I remember I told him Papa was on his way to bring him home.

That night I would have to tell Tain his friend Ben had died. That night and in the weeks and months to come I would have to hold the space for him. I continue to hold it so Tain can see there is room, always room, even when death has entered, for life— for what comes next, for what we need to do to comfort Fran, a mother who can no longer hold such a space for her lost son.

Think of the wingspan required to hold such a space. Think of how the space must be as broad and deep as the path you hope is open to any child of the world. Think of what such a task asks of your body and being and what it means to hold onto a promise that was never spoken aloud. Now you have your answer and so do I. All this is why I didn't go to the firehouse.

FOR ROXANE GAY

NOTES FROM A FORGIVING HEART

A few days ago a friend made a kind and generous offer: if I wanted to write about Charleston, about my feelings about the shooting and about community tragedy in general, she would post it and promote it. I declined. I told her it seemed plenty of people were having their say and I had nothing to add. But I wasn't being entirely truthful.

The real reason I turned her down was this: to write about Charleston I would have to write about December 14, 2012. I would have to write about Sandy Hook Elementary where my son, then in third grade, hid under a table in his classroom while down the hall his godbrother and many others he cared about were murdered by Adam Lanza. I couldn't write about it then. Couldn't write about it now.

However, Roxane Gay's *New York Times* piece "Why I Can't Forgive Dylann Roof" has unlocked something in me. Her voice is powerful, bright, and clear like a clarion full-blown in tone and meaning. But her adamant stance against forgiveness struck a dissonant note so jarring it drove me to pick up my pen.

I'm not going to sit here and say Ms. Gay must forgive Dylann Roof. But because she writes, "I cannot fathom how they (the families of the Charleston victims) are capable of such eloquent mercy," I am impelled to respond. I know many others are similarly flummoxed. I do want her and everyone else to understand this forgiveness and why it's important.

I'll begin here, with this part of Ms. Gay's essay: "My lack of forgiveness serves as a reminder that there are some acts that are so terrible that we should recognize them as such. We should recognize them as beyond forgiving."

Forgiveness doesn't mean you don't recognize the evil. On the contrary—forgiveness recognizes the evil and also the vital necessity that we must face evil full on. The recognition alerts us to work that must be done and we have to figure out what that work is, what personal gifts must be brought to bear to maintain the light so the darkness does not overcome us. But you can't do all the work you need to do if you are tied up in an unforgiving state. Ms. Gay writes, "My unwillingness to forgive this man does not give him any kind of power."

Dylann Roof may be, as she says, "beneath my contempt," but even to place him as such means he gets to stay within you. He gets to take up residence like a tiger stalking back and forth between your heart and mind. And with this trespasser so present, what does one do? You stand in the cage with your whip and chair at the ready, ever vigilant, waiting to do battle the moment the hate and anger begin to claw at your heart once more.

But here's the thing: while you're doing that, the rest of your life goes unlived. You don't tend to your family and your gifts. You forget how to experience joy.

I think this is why forgiveness shows up in the Bible in the first place. When Jesus is asked how many times we should forgive he answers, "Not seven times but, I tell you, seventy-seven times" (Matthew 18:22). Why?

Because God wanted to warn us against anything that would divide us from ourselves—from our families, our friends, and from knowing our own right minds. Even if you're a person who doesn't believe in God, let's agree that these are all good and desirable things. We don't wish to be separated. "A house divided against itself cannot stand." We want to stay whole.

So forgiveness is not for Dylann Roof and it's not to ease society or any white guilt for the racism so prevalent. The forgiveness is for you. You need it because a hole has been rent open in your life. It will take all your heart, all your energy, and all your focus to step through it and figure out what your life is now—the so-called new normal. Without forgiveness you stay frozen in the moment. Frozen means stuck, no movement, no life.

If I had stayed frozen in anger and grief I would have missed the signs of my son telling me exactly what he needed to grieve his godbrother after the Sandy Hook shooting. I would have been impatient with his requests. He asked for pictures of him and his friend together that he could attach to the clothing he would wear to the funeral. When he saw the tall glass candles with pictures of his friend decorating the tables and wanted one, I asked and made sure he could take one home. It sits by his bedside to this very day.

These acts may seem small, but what would have happened if I had been too angry and unforgiving, too focused on Adam Lanza? I would have been impatient, too busy hopping from one hot spot to the next. I would have told my son, "You don't need that. I don't have time to print pictures. Put that candle down, it's not yours." What knot of frustration and anger would have formed in him then? How many times would I have betrayed him, failed him, before realizing the damage that could not be undone?

The weekend of the Sandy Hook shooting I taught my scheduled Sunday school class for the third graders at Trinity Episcopal Church. The room was packed with children, more than the usual number, as well as their parents who stayed with them. I sat on a tiny plastic chair, a Bible open across my lap, my son sitting next to me. A reporter later asked how I could do that, how could I teach a Sunday school class just two days after the tragedy? I told him I had to, because people needed it. The packed room was proof of that. I knew I had to be present, very present, in order to help, to focus on the lesson.

I explained how the previous week we had done a project, based on John Lennon's song "Imagine," in which we made posters imagining what we wanted the world to be like. Of course, being third graders, they wanted no homework and lots of candy. But they also wanted no killing. And they wanted people to be nice to each other. We hung the posters in the hallway. I told the reporter I taught Sunday school that day because the children needed to know the world they imagine is still possible. But I can't authentically deliver that message if there is a barrier of unforgiveness keeping me from believing it myself.

By the way, about the media . . . Ms. Gay wrote, "The dominant media narrative vigorously embraced the notion of forgiveness, seeming to believe that if we forgive we have somehow found a way to make sense of the incomprehensible." But forgiveness is not about having the Charleston shooting make sense. It's about refusing to allow it to damage our lives more than it already has. When Nadine Collier made her statement about the loss of her mother, I heard a strong woman recognizing the path she must now walk. She released Dylann Roof to walk his own path so he would not continue to tread on hers.

I also don't agree with Ms. Gay's statement that "Black people forgive because we need to survive." Forgiveness is too difficult. Why would we cross that bridge, tax our hearts, for the constricted, miniscule, poor result of "survival"? It is too little recompense for such arduous work. Besides, as Andy Andrews observes in his book *The Traveler's Gift*, we aren't meant to scratch at the ground like chickens trying to survive. We are meant to soar like eagles. We are meant to have life and to have it abundantly. And we are meant to have peace within ourselves. As Jesus said, *Peace I leave with you; my peace I give to you. I do not give to you as the world gives. Do not let your hearts be troubled, and do not let them be afraid* (John 14:27).

This is a tremendous gift. But a gift must be accepted and held. When we do not forgive we forfeit this gift. We need to forgive so we can still have a vision of a better world. The shootings in Sandy Hook and now Charleston are grim reminders that we are far from it, but not forgiving will take us even further away. We would remain stuck. We would remain traumatized, whether we realize it or not. Unless we choose to be the light in the world, as Ms. Collier and others like her have done, we succumb to the darkness. When we don't forgive the victim count grows, and can grow exponentially. Adam Lanza took twenty-seven. Dylann Roof took nine. *They don't get to take any more.* That's why forgiveness matters.

PART TWO

HOLDING
ONE END OF A LOVE

UPBRINGING

---

*T*he essay I wrote for my Introduction to Rhetoric class in college started like this:

My father was raised on a farm in Mississippi in the 1920s. He grew up with the rod, along with his thirteen siblings. You worked as soon as you were old enough, and either parent 'went upside your head' if you misbehaved or did any of your work unsatisfactorily. My father thought nothing of raising us in the same way. As soon as we were old enough to put a chair up to the sink or stove we were expected to wash dishes and cook meals. Under any other circumstances I would not have minded because when I started school I found that these were things other kids my age did not normally do. I thought I was clever to be so capable in the kitchen. However the pain that accompanied this experience was not worth it. "Whippins" were a common part of my life. My father hit us with switches, electric cords, fan belts, his belt, whatever phase he happened to be going through, whatever he could get his hands on the fastest. The only thing I knew for sure was that it hurt. We were left with red marks on our arms and

legs, and faces, if his aim happened to be poor or we were mov-
ing around too much. He didn't like hitting our faces. I used to
think it was because he didn't want evidence people could see.

I once deemed this piece the story of my life. I wrote it when I
was twenty years old for an expository writing class called "Introduction to Rhetoric." The assignment: write an autobiographical
essay. At the time, now over twenty-five years ago, I had no aspi-
rations to be a writer—I had no concept of such a thing, and I
was still struggling along with organic chemistry, neurobiology,
and all the other unromantic courses one took when planning to
apply to medical school. But I had been writing since childhood
and I carried with me some vague notion that I should keep writing so I registered for this class that required its students to sub-
mit five pages of new work each week, to be discussed one-on-one
with a member of the writing faculty. When the assignment came
up I had to make a choice that, though I didn't realize it at the
time, would shape my future writing life. The question I asked
myself was this: would I tell the truth about my upbringing, or
would I make something up, something that would be acceptable to my parents if the essay somehow found its way into their
hands? In this first paragraph—and I'm shocked to read it today
and see how quickly I jumped all the way in—I decided to tell
the truth. "Did your father hit you?" a friend once asked me. My
answer was and is, "Yes," and the paragraph above is, I think, a
straightforward depiction of how this happened and why I took
issue with it. I was probably also coming to the understanding
that this didn't make my childhood unique, but I would write out
once and for all the answer to the question and I wouldn't be sen-
timental about it.

Of course I know "truth" can be a tricky thing and is often
in the eye of the beholder. So I will say this essay represented
the truth as I knew it then. I come back to it now because I
once believed I would never write about my upbringing again. I
thought I had said the one true thing about what I had lived and
what I learned. But I've recently come to see it is necessary for me
to look at this essay again, to discuss it again. I'm realizing now
that, despite my father's death in 1991, so much of what I write

happens with this essay in mind. I am either in dialogue with it, or I am seeking to protect what I built in myself when I wrote it. Whatever I write about myself now and in the years to come, the story will always start here. I see no way around it.

I had always thought that the less I thought about my home life, the less pain I would feel. I brought home tons of books from the library—books about girls my age who had loving parents and interesting lives. I let myself get caught up in their proms, vacations, and daydreams. It was those books that showed me that not everyone lived as we did, that everyone else's parents didn't hit them. My father used to say it was because we weren't as good or as clean. But I didn't see any difference between me and those other girls. I could imagine myself into their places, and I seemed to fit in perfectly. Daydreaming was a cheap escape, but I indulged because I knew no other comfort. I remember thinking about the storybook girls as I leaned into the kitchen sink, up to my elbows in dirty dishwater. I would sort of laugh to myself because I knew I saw a world inside of my head that my parents could not enter.

However, I was not content to have that world only in my head. There was a place for me in the world outside of my parents' lives. My oldest brother had proved that when I was nine by leaving for college; he never permanently lived with us again. He had achieved a freedom that I had never thought was possible. Therefore college became the ultimate answer. But I had years to go before I could attain that goal, and in those years I learned caution and patience. Caution because I tried everything in my power, from staying up late washing the final dishes to keeping my father out of the refrigerator when it was too dirty, to keep him from getting upset. I learned patience because these things did not always work, and I knew there were many more whippins to endure before I was old enough for college. But the thought lingered quietly in my mind. It was my own private solace as I defrosted freezers, washed windows, and cleaned. But when I was whipped, the thoughts became fierce determination as I clenched my fists and fought back tears. Someday they would never touch me again.

If I am to properly engage this essay from the past I must begin by absolving myself of the imperfect craft technique I once exhibited, or else my head will be warped from cringing. I have to forgive myself, for example, for the terrible number of times the word "was" appears in my old writing. I must remind myself I wrote in the best way I knew then just as I put forth my best effort in each piece I write now. I don't want to be a writer who dislikes encountering her early work. But in order for me to do that I must be honest with myself about the effort (did I give it my all or was I rushing to meet a deadline?) and I must be open to forgiveness.

Aside from that, I look at these paragraphs and remember how I've forgotten many of the skills my father taught me because I have no use for them. Once upon a time many Lake Erie specimens passed under my hands as my siblings and I sat in our backyard in Lorain, Ohio, scaling and gutting the fish packed in boxes of crushed ice that my father bought from the local fishermen. I haven't scaled a fish since college when, as a stage manager working on a production of Sam Shepherd one-act plays, *Suicide in B-Flat* and *Action,* I instructed one of the *Action* actors on how to clean a fish so he could do so onstage as the script called for. As soon as I got to my room that night I called my father and related the whole scene to him.

"Really, Fronia?" he asked, astonished. "Those people up there don't know how to clean fish?"

"No, Daddy, they don't!"

"Well, I'll be damned."

I smile recalling how delighted I was at his surprise, despite our wacky and mistaken generalization of the whole of Massachusetts. My father and I shared few points of connection. I should think about this phone call more often, allow it to warm my soul and tend the space in my heart where his memory resides. I read somewhere that the dead, wherever they have gone, awaken and live again each time we think about them. I feel this memory might work that wonder for my father.

These paragraphs also remind me of how I learned patience and a focused work ethic. Such traits, imprinted on me so deep the ink can never fade, are what I'm unwilling to sacrifice if granted the wish to have grown up another way. With patience and work I know how to survive: I do my work—back then it was schoolwork—and if I'm in an unsatisfactory situation, as I was then, I am patient and watchful, looking for the opportunity to take action when a favorable shift occurs. I don't mind if I'm waiting for years because my childhood made me acutely aware that change often requires years. I am more concerned with what I'm doing during this waiting time because the work, the activity I do while I'm waiting, will leave its mark on me—writing letters when separated from loved ones, practicing yoga during infertility treatments and pregnancy, reading travel guides while saving up for a trip. I think I spent most of my childhood waiting time writing, reading, observing, preparing. Recently I read an academic article that referred to patience as "immersive attention" and discussed the virtues of teaching students to slow down and value the power of observation. If that were a class when I was in school I would have been able to test out of it. I've got the patience thing down cold.

There were many times when I considered a drastic alternative: running away. But that was when the situation was particularly drastic. Those were usually times when something important was missing in the house, for instance, my father's wallet or a set of keys. Keys were important because everything in the house was locked up: my parents' room, my father's toolboxes, the telephone, and even the refrigerator. My father was always accusing us of stealing things to give or sell to our neighbors. He would threaten to take us to the county detention home. I saw it as a major threat to my plans because kids in the detention home didn't go to school. School was the only real life I had because there, for six hours a day, I could be like all the other kids. It was also a major step in my journey towards college, so when I stood to lose school I made up long intricate plans for running away. I left windows cracked open so I could get inside the house in case I ran away from the parking lot of the home. I could get my clothes and leave before they caught me. I thought of friends' houses where I could stay. I didn't think I would have any problems. Who would turn away a child who only wanted to go to school? But later on I realized that running away could only make things worse for me. I knew I couldn't convince anyone of my father's maltreatment because he could convince anyone that we deserved it. I had seen him do so before. I saw myself getting caught in red tape, being placed in a foster home, and missing lots of school.

I really couldn't write about the above now if I had to explain my life. I have released so many of these details and feelings from my mind, like an armful of leaves I've thrown into a river. They floated away from me so long ago. If I tried to gather them today in the same way, the same detail, I think there would be a certain melodrama attached to it. I see myself running fast beside the river, net in hand, trying to recapture the leaves. I am breathless over what I managed to gather, distraught over what I may have missed, but constantly running despite the imperfect effort. Mary Johnson, the author of the memoir *An Unquenchable Thirst*, said in a workshop I once attended that in order to write memoir you must spend a good deal of time remembering. I agree with this, but I also know that at any given point in your life you are a different person doing the remembering. I am fortunate. This old essay is a gift to myself because I know I would not have remembered so many of the details of my childhood, at least not in this way. In fact, I've let so much of it go because I thought it didn't matter anymore. I'm not sure I would have been able to access the detail of a locked refrigerator now without trying to make it into a joke.

I do find this line intriguing: "Who would turn away a child who only wanted to go to school?" It sounds like I thought I wasn't asking for much—give me a bed, a few meals, and show me where to catch the bus in the morning and I'll be fine. I think the "fierce determination" I referenced earlier molded me into something of an independent spirit, one that didn't seek affection probably because at the time so many other pieces that were important to me—safety, peace of mind, an education—came first in my hierarchy of human needs. As I consider it now I remember how this trait carried over into college, how I enjoyed meeting new people and making friends, but didn't really allow too many to get close to me. I don't believe this was intentional, I just didn't know any other way to be. I never gave hugs, and I received them awkwardly because I had little experience with them. This is so far from the way I am now, an expert hugger in my adoration of friends I dearly love, that I want to throw my arms around this twenty-year-old version of me. She's seriously in need of a hug.

My father looked imposing. When I would try to describe him to people, they would hear that he was only 5'10", and say that that did not sound scary. But anyone who saw him understood. For being only 5'10" he was a big man. His arms were so thick that ordinary shirts did not fit him. He ordered his clothes from King Size catalogs. He used to dress mainly in his work clothes from U.S. Steel where he worked as the foreman in the galvanizing department. Once he retired (because of a heart condition) he dressed in white dress shirts with a tie and slacks. To him, it was always good to look as if you had money. So he wore it. His belt buckle sported a mass of silver dollars and quarters that he had welded on himself. He also wore silver dollars on his shoes, and made tiepins out of dimes. On his right hand was a ring he made out of an 1880 quarter.

The skin on his hands was rough, more like hide than skin. His fingers had rounded fingertips with fingernails that he kept cut very short. The skin of his face sagged. I can never recall him being young since he was almost fifty when I was born. (I was the third of seven, coming after my two brothers, and the oldest of the five girls.) His eyes were lively and wild, fiercely animating his face when he spoke. The nose on his face was a wide triangle. His lips were moderately thick, but the width of his mouth compensated for that. The mouth was partially toothless, the teeth rotting and falling out from time to time. But the teeth that remained were strong. His voice had a rough tone, and the lack of teeth made it difficult for him to be understood on the phone. The only time his voice sounded clear was when he sang. It was the only time he didn't really scare me, because I was assured that he was in a good mood.

Oh my Daddy. This reminds me of how he was a mountain to me. Once, when I was about nine, he stumbled coming down the front steps of his sister's house and hit the ground hard. I stood nearby and I swear I felt the impact of the blow beneath my feet. Blood trickled down the side of his face. Ultimately, he was fine, but I felt frightened and disoriented because in that moment the world made no sense. The biggest landmark of my life, the one that was always steadfast, as present and reliable as the sun, had fallen. I probably realized then that as much as I feared him, I could not understand a world without him. I remember him asking me to scratch his back and how, shoulder-to-shoulder, it seemed broad enough to fit a map of the world. I think I was proud of my father's size in a "my dad can kick your dad's butt" kind of way. This physical aspect of him I miss the most because when he was in a good mood, singing and lighting up a King Edward cigar, which he liked to smoke when taking breaks from his Pall Mall cigarettes, I did feel safe in the shadow of his mountain. Three years after the essay I wrote in college was published, lung cancer quickly stripped him of his weight and energy. He died at the age of 71. If I'm walking down a crowded street in Manhattan and catch the scent of a good cigar, my head still whips around in search of him or rather the memory of his weighty presence, his security. My father has substance even in my dreams where he appears as real and heavy as in my childhood. The words "ethereal" or "ghost" are just too light for Daddy.

No one ever went against him or doubted his word. If in a particular month he could not pay the phone bill, he would just go downtown, march into the office, and ask for the head manager. Then he would go into his speech about working for U.S. Steel for 34 years and being disabled for his bad heart and having seven kids to feed. (He would say seven even when my brothers weren't living at home. I used to think it was because he counted my mother also.) The amazing thing is that the manager would say it was all right, that Mr. Scott was one of their best customers, and that he didn't have to worry about the phone being turned off. It was things like that that made my father feel all the more high and mighty. I used to think he could get away with murder in that city. If he was like that about the phone bill, there was no way anyone would challenge him for mistreating his children. Once my oldest brother, after my second brother received a severe beating, sent the police to our house. It was a small seven-room house, but it and our front and back yards were thoroughly surrounded by a five-foot high chain link fence. The policemen looked at the padlock on the gate, shook their heads, and left. A social worker that was sent later sided with my father and the whole ordeal was supposedly settled before we came home from school. He brags about it to this day. I lost faith in the "outside world" and stopped believing that some nice person would save us someday. I gave up, and thought our situation to be hopeless.

When my father spoke, people listened. I think they got the sense that he was a man who didn't waste words because if anyone saw him in public, he wasn't talking. He sat quietly in the parking lot listening to the radio while we shopped with our mother in the stores or while she attended our teacher conferences. He didn't like public places, and the one or two times my siblings saw him in our school—for instance when he responded in person to the band director's phone call after my sister Theodora didn't turn in her money from a fundraiser on time—we nearly collapsed in the hallway for fear of what one of us had done to draw his presence into unfamiliar territory. At home, though, and to his friends, he could monologue so long and so well you'd think he'd stepped out of an August Wilson play. His stories, usually involving women, employers, drunk men, and sometimes guns, became the litany my siblings and I could recite by heart.

The "outside world" deserves more credit than I gave it. The right interventions did arrive, only in ways I didn't expect. One came on the day my mother and I went to see Attorney Gordon, as we called him, the lawyer my father always used to help with paperwork pertaining to the Social Security and disability benefits he started receiving after he had a heart attack and retired from the steel mill. Actually, Attorney Gordon assisted with anything that required a signature—an essential service because my father was illiterate. That day—it was the summer before my senior year in high school—as he looked over whatever papers my mother handed him, Attorney Gordon asked me where I would apply for college. I mentioned Ohio State and Syracuse as possibilities.

"Why are you applying to those schools? With your grades you could go to school out East."

"Where would I get the money?" I said.

And then, the miraculous sentences that changed my life:

"It would be cheaper for you to go to school out East because those schools have more money to give. They have plenty of students from families who can afford to pay so there's more available for financial aid. If you go to a school like Ohio State, everybody needs help and there's not enough to go around. There's money out East for you; all you have to do is get in."

I trusted Attorney Gordon knew what he was talking about—he had his own Ivy League shingle, from Yale, on his wall. And I may have even stared at it again, as I'd done many times sitting in that office, before saying to him, "Okay."

Once I did get accepted to schools and decided to go to Harvard, I had to appeal to Attorney Gordon again—my father refused to let me sign and return the card indicating I agreed to enroll. He worried I was committing him to spending money he didn't have. But the lawyer assured Daddy that my getting into this school was a good thing, it was one of the best in the country in fact, and I had been offered an excellent financial aid package.

"All right then," my father said.

Therefore I endured. I had no other choice. When I got to junior high I became involved in as many extracurricular activities as possible. The more hours I could stay after school, the better. Then I would come home, read, do homework, and wait to turn eighteen. I thought I was surviving, building a good academic reputation, and awaiting a bright future. But actually I was accumulating a kind of bitterness, not unlike that of a caged animal. I realized this when my father would buy something I needed for school like basketball shoes or poster board. He would or wouldn't complain, depending on his mood. But either way I knew he did it because he thought it was his duty as a father to supply such needs. And although I didn't show it, I thought the whole thing was a hypocritical charade. How could he treat us like slaves and then put on this show of being a great father? I did my best to ask for as little as possible. I didn't want to be part of the charade so I only asked for things when they were monetarily out of my reach and I needed them badly. But then he would make such a noisy fuss that I believe I paid dearly for my self-betrayal.

Three words here laden with the darkness I didn't know I needed to slough off: bitterness, slaves, and betrayal. Together they tell a story that isn't written here. I'll start with "slaves" because at age twenty I should have known better than to wield this ugly word, to understand it conjures a hundred different kinds of hurt and melodrama that didn't belong in that essay. But I also know I did not use it casually, that I had given in to the eight-year-old version of myself standing over me as I wrote and shaking a fist at an old wrong. At eight I was bold enough to complain to my mother about Daddy's treatment of us and I said we were like slaves. And I did mean "us" because he hit her too though not as often. I thought we were in the same situation, but her being the adult she could make some sense of it for me. I don't remember her response or if she even responded, perhaps because I recall all too well how she acted—she told Daddy what I'd said. For the next week, maybe longer, he poured out a constant stream of justifications, about how my siblings and I didn't know how to behave or keep the house clean, how I didn't know what a real whipping was. He probably also made awful comments about my features too. He used to call me a yellow-skinned bastard. Why? I honestly have no idea. I heard the word "bastard" a lot growing up but I knew it only as a swear word and didn't think it was any different than the word "bitch." I never thought about it inferring a question of legitimacy until, in a more recent essay, I mentioned my father saying this and one of my readers asked if Daddy thought he wasn't my father. It never occurred to me because my father would say this hurtful thing about my features one day, and then the next he would be bragging about how my red hair comes from his side of the family—and I felt this to be true even though I was the only one of his seven children born with this hair and I only met the throng of my older redheaded cousins, who mostly live in St. Louis, after my father's death.

I don't think I received a whipping for saying he treated us like slaves—I would have been relieved if I did and Daddy left it at that. But through it all, I think I felt more humiliated by my mother's betrayal. I don't even remember all the things my father said in those days, but I do remember her just sitting there, small and silent. I may sound melodramatic, but this is true: I didn't confide in her about him ever again. As a child taught to believe adults knew best, I'm sure I felt frustrated by my mother's behavior, and my father's. I wanted to believe they should have known better, that if someone—that person being me—pointed out to them how sad and terrible the situation in our home was that they would just snap out of it and do what was right, despite me having no idea what would be "right." I guess that's where the bitterness came in as well. I just wanted to believe they could change and not be the way they were. I suppose I wanted them to have a kind of awareness about us, about their children, and felt cheated when I knew for certain it so obviously wasn't there.

I remember having packed every possession I had when I left for college—every poster, every little odd and end that I specifically had saved for college since I was thirteen. My time had finally come, and I packed everything because I had no intention of returning. I remember feeling very bitter: it was a sour, acrid feeling that churned in me, mixing with the excitement and anticipation I felt for the journey ahead of me. I sat on the arm of an armchair, awaiting the arrival of my brother and his wife, who would drive me there. My parents had left to take one of my sisters to school for a football game. They said they would try to be back before I left. I sat there thinking I really didn't care if they weren't back in time.

They treated my brothers as if they were princes once they left home. I always thought it was because they had to. If they didn't, my brothers didn't have to come home. But for some reason they always did come home. I couldn't understand it. Had they really forgotten all that had happened to us? I listened to the conversations they had with our father in sheer disbelief. He spoke to them as if they were men visiting his house. He would describe recent events or accessories he had bought for the van;

he even told them about the whippings he gave us for assorted wrongdoings, always ending his story with, "Now was I right or wrong?" to which my brothers would always answer, "Yes, sir, you were right." He would also tell stories of his life, which we had all heard over and over again throughout the course of our own lives. In the kitchen my sisters and I would listen to them conjuring up fake laughter to go along with my father's laughing at stories he thought were still funny. My sisters and I laughed at all of them.

I could never forgive them like that, I thought, as I looked at my boxes and luggage taking up most of the space in the tiny living room. I felt as if I were the ten-year-old Jane Eyre being whisked away to her boarding school. Like her, I sought refuge, a new home. It upset me that home had never been my home. It had been a desolate holding pen where I had lived, biding my time, waiting for my turn to leave. My parents did not really know me so I didn't believe they could truly miss me. The frustration I felt because of that only made me more bitter so I just sat there and tried to think of nothing. They did return in time for my departure. My father insisted on overseeing the tying of my bike onto the back of my brother's car. With great difficulty, I made him put a twenty-dollar bill he had tried to give me back into his pocket. I told him I had enough money.

I think the paradox, or what I saw then as the hypocrisy of my father, bothered me the most. I wanted to resolve it in my mind. It seemed to me he had to be all loving or all lousy—I couldn't understand, nor wanted, him to be both at once. If he were just mean I could write him off and live estranged from him and be content to do so. But I couldn't resolve this with the love I did see in him and tried very hard to ignore—his determination to get that bike for me, which he finally did on credit, from a local shop; how he practically went out of his mind with worry in the fall of 1985 when I called home to tell him where I would hunker down for Hurricane Gloria—with no sense of geography he didn't know until that moment my school was in the path of the storm he'd been hearing about on the evening news. The contradictions of Daddy sat firm like a doorstop to the opening of my heart, allowing the required space—and I think I needed only a little—for forgiveness to nudge its way in.

It wasn't long before my roommates noticed I didn't have a close relationship with my parents. I rarely called home, and I never asked them for anything. I paid my own bills and bought my own books. I never spoke of them because for a while it all still seemed to be unspeakable. I was still of the mind that no one would believe me, and I also didn't see how it mattered to anyone how I was brought up. However, one of the things I learned at college was that your friends can care so much they want to know all about you, and so it was that I ended up describing my upbringing to one of my roommates. Afterwards she asked something I had never thought about before. She asked, "Why did he do it?" I remember staring at her and wanting, with all my heart, to tell her that I didn't know. But in the back of my mind I knew that I did know. Once my father, after whipping one of my sisters, had said heatedly to himself, "I gots to whip her 'cause if I don't, she won't think she done anything wrong. Youse got to keep after these people here." I had ignored it, brushing it off as a flimsy excuse for his temper, but as I sat there thinking about his own uneducated upbringing in Mississippi I realized that he had raised us in the only way he knew how. He never saw any wrong in hitting us because he had been hit in the same way. The fact that we were growing up to be respectable students and human beings only proved to him that he had been right. If given the chance, he would raise us the same way all over again.

I called home and listened to my father ramble on about the van and the weather. He only listened to me long enough to hear me say that I was "fine, Daddy." He would go on about how he had the prettiest and smartest girls in school, and how he showed my picture to everyone he met saying, "This is my girl that goes to Hartford,' and how they would read the window stickers on the van, and know he really meant Harvard. "Yes, Daddy. Really, Daddy? Yes, sir, Daddy, they have that here. I'm fine, Daddy." I sat there, with the phone to my ear, crying silently because he really didn't know what he had done to us. He knew nothing of

the hate or the pain and bitterness I had felt. It was like hating an
innocent child, so it seemed pointless to feel it all anymore.

And here it is. Coming to these words over twenty-five years
ago changed my life. They didn't arrive on the paper easily, certainly not as easily as it reads to me now. I resisted them. My husband, whom I met while I was still in college, once told me that
I was so much like my father that if I didn't come to understand
him I would never really know myself. Of course I didn't want to
think I was anything like him but it was all there, even then: the
introvert who is content to avoid large gatherings but can also be
an engaging extrovert when the situation requires it; a work ethic
and focus as strong as the steel he once worked in the local mill;
and yes, an ability to love even if we're not always successful in
knowing how to show it. I am my father's daughter. I can believe
that truth without remorse, and I can understand the importance
of forgiveness because of the contemplation that led me to write
these words so many years ago. These words granted me time in
which to feel this forgiveness in his presence before he died. But
then, as they say, forgiveness is never about the person you're forgiving. It's a gift for you. In forgiving my father I put down what
felt like a suitcase full of granite. I walked lighter after that. I used
to think it was because I didn't have all that anger simmering in
me. Now I think my buoyance came from knowing for certain—
and accepting—that my father loved me.

A FUR FOR ANNIE PEARL

T he old woman's hips seemed to be spring-loaded. I didn't know how else she was able to jump off her little house's porch and come at me so fast, her legs pumping in a speed walk that seemed to be her way of trying to remember how to run.

"My baby! My baby's come back! I knew she'd come, I just knew it!"

The eyes behind her bifocals radiated joy and her arms, thrown open, soon clasped around my neck. These arms were thick but powerful and it felt like someone had laid a boa constrictor over me. Her bristly chin scraped the skin of my bare shoulder. Confusion overwhelmed me. She laughed—I did not know this woman! I managed an uneasy smile, but within minutes I was prepared to give her anything she asked for because of what she said next, and because of what those words gave to me.

When she released me she spoke in short, excited sentences that were barely sentences and she shook her index finger at me to accentuate each one.

"Your father! Vassie Scott! Pulled up here in that car right after you were born! He came to me with you in his arms—like this!" She clutched the floral print apron tied around the waist of her short-sleeved pink polyester dress, rolled up the fabric and tucked it into the crook of her left arm. "He said, 'Pearl! I've got something for you!' And it was YOU! You were just the prettiest thing I'd ever seen and I just kept hugging you and kissing you!" She laughed and slapped her thigh. "And your Daddy says, (she pushed her vocal cords to a lower register in perfect imitation of the voice I recognized at once) 'Pearl, gimme my baby back here before you eat her up!'"

I processed her words as quickly as I could but my brain seemed slow as though its hard drive had crashed and needed rebooting. This woman literally blew my mind—*Daddy, his baby, me!*

I try to conjure the image, a golden one because of its newness and surprise—me as an infant in my father's arms. I have only one picture of me as a baby. It is a small, wallet-sized photograph, black and white, taken by the hospital photographer just hours after I was born. In this image I am a tiny head, eyes closed, with a big tuft of hair on top. The rest of me disappears into the white blankets swaddling my tiny being. I've never seen a picture of either of my parents holding me, the third of what would be seven children, but the first girl. When I think about how this story, specifically its choreographing, may have come about it is even more amazing to me. My mother must have been holding me—this was 1966, the time before infant car seats—and she did not drive. So my father, for this story to play out the way I've been told, must have pulled up in front of the house and taken me from my mother's arms. He did it so he could present me with pride to his friend. I wondered what my brothers, aged 9 and 2, were doing in the car while this was happening. I know they must have been there—my father didn't believe in babysitters or in leaving children home alone until one of us reached the age of 12. Did my brothers have to sit through this scene more than once that day at various friends' houses? The thought fascinated me and it still does. This stranger, Annie Pearl Charleston, had given me a tremendous gift and she tossed it out so happily and easily, like a wealthy woman in a fairy tale flinging gold coins into the street. I fell to my knees gathering them, not realizing until that moment the depth of my emotional hunger.

As Annie Pearl laughed and hugged me again, my mother got out of my rental car and stood looking very pleased. She had delivered the goods, though it had taken months of prodding to do it. She began her campaign not long after my father's death in 1991. She would call me at work and speak to me as if Lorain, Ohio, were just around the corner from my office in midtown Manhattan.

"Annie Pearl says she wants to see you."

"Mom, I don't know Annie Pearl."

"Yes you do. She lives over there on West 21st Street."

When I was a child my parents—I should say my father, because he spearheaded the excursions—took us visiting often. They would pile all seven kids into the station wagon and we would drive around Lorain and sometimes to Elyria. Most of the people we visited were relatives—both of my parents had siblings nearby and my mother's father lived in Elyria. But we also called on friends and I remember the names of all the non-relatives we saw regularly: Doll, Mattie, Miss Mary, Miss Regina and her brother Mr. Walt, Mr. and Mrs. Frisbee, Mr. Buster (real name Henry Williams), and Bertha Mae. After my father died his many friends and relatives materialized out of the vapor of my childhood memory to pay their respects. Even if I'd never seen some of them before, I still knew who they were. Daddy was a talker who told stories endlessly, often telling the same ones repeatedly, so I would hear a name and be able to place them in the map of my father's life: He knew this person in St. Louis, that man worked with him at the steel mill, this woman used to be married to a brother long deceased. I had no memory of anyone named Annie Pearl.

"Well, she had some falling out with your daddy," my mother said in that halting way she had of speaking when she didn't remember the pertinent details or, and this was probably closer to the truth, she didn't understand what happened at the time. Either way, this didn't strengthen her argument.

If it had been my father doing the asking . . . well, there would have been no asking. I would have been sitting in our living room listening to him talk as was my custom for visiting him ever since I left home for college. He would have commanded as if just in that moment he had made up his mind to do so, "Let's go on up here and see Annie Pearl."

"Yes, sir."

The point is we would have gone, and I would have done so obediently. There was a time though when I would have gone with resentment in my heart because, the truth is, I had a falling out with my daddy too, although neither he nor my mother would have recognized it as such. My father was a commander but when commanding failed, he hit us, my mother included. He would lash out with electric cords or dryer belts, sometimes even beating us out of bed in the middle of the night because we'd left dishes unwashed in the kitchen sink. I rarely think about or discuss this anymore because when I moved away and could view my family from a distance—and become more exposed to the experience of others—I came to understand my father raised us in a way that he and many others of his age and culture brought up their off-spring. I'm one of a whole population of children who were sent into the woods to fetch the switches for their own whippings.

But what remains in me, and what I am constantly encountering, years later, are the emotional marks still left in me that need to be smoothed, nursed, comforted. When I came to forgive and understand my father all I could do was visit him, sit and listen, knowing he would never throw his arms around me and say he loved me. That just wasn't who he was. So I began looking for the signs of love in his past and present actions. Like the time just before I went to college when he took me to a bike shop we regularly patronized and talked the owner into giving me a new bike at a significant discount, which he would pay over time because "that child is going away to school and needs some way of getting around." That bike, a basic women's three-speed, was stolen before my senior year. I remember being too tired to carry it up the four flights of stairs where I was living that summer. I left it locked to a telephone pole near the front door, but the next morning I found the cable cut and my bike was gone. My roommates didn't understand why I cried so hard, why I was inconsolable. I still think of it when I see bikes cabled to telephone poles or parking meters. Not because of the bike itself, but because it represented a tangible sign of my father's love. Whenever I would uncover these signs of love in my memories or in something he did, I would call him or travel to see him and deliver a silent thanks. It had to be silent because he did all the talking, but to hear him was another kind of gift. I could tell by his warm and lofty tones that he was glad to be in touch with me.

I thought I found all the gifts and, after he died, there would be no more signs of love. But Annie Pearl offered me another—shiny, bright, and precious. I cherish the image of my father holding me in his arms. I would have been days old, full of fresh baby scent, probably only a little bigger than the apron material bunched up in Annie Pearl's hands.

That afternoon with Annie Pearl I learned she had known my father even before he was married to my mother. She lived in the same rooming house as he did near the steel mill.

"He was a real quiet man, just kept to himself, listening to his blues records in his room," she said. "Then there was that night they went to messing with him." She didn't say who "they" were but I assumed she meant some assembled men, perhaps co-workers, sitting around playing cards, getting bored, and, as some men will do, looking to pick on someone.

My father was not someone to pick on. I knew that, of course, and Annie Pearl quickly confirmed it.

"He took that man and threw him into the stove! I had spaghetti all over me!" Her hands fluttered up and down her torso as if she were still surveying the mess on her clothes. "But they never bothered him again!"

Yes, that sounded like my daddy.

There was something exhilarating about the stories Annie Pearl told me. I felt alive, baptized, as though she poured water over my head and confirmed something I once thought I believed but in reality only hoped to believe—my father loved me. And I could trust the stories she told because she didn't paint a beatific portrait of him. She saw both sides of my father, his violence and his love, and could reconcile and accept both.

My mother and I sat in Annie Pearl's house—it had that musty smell of a place lived in for decades. I, struck by Annie Pearl's youthful movement and energy, asked her age. "I'm seventy-eight years old! Can you believe that?" She laughed as though she couldn't believe it herself.

"No! I don't believe that."

At some point in the afternoon she leaned toward me, almost conspiratorially.

"You live in New York City, right?"

"Yes, ma'am, I do."

"Is there any way you can get me one of them furs the women there wear? I've always wanted me one. I see them on TV, women in New York City, walking down the street in fur coats!"

I saw the television show *The Jeffersons* playing on a screen in my memory and Louise Jefferson, as played by Isabel Sanford, coming through the door of her—as the theme song went—East Side apartment in the sky, removing her fur coat and handing it to Florence the maid. Annie Pearl could have seen other fur-clad females in soap operas or old Hollywood movies, just as I have, but the keywords—women, New York, fur—coming from her brought up Louise Jefferson and I, that quickly, made up the story for myself that she was the person Annie Pearl wanted to emulate.

"Wow, that's a great idea!" I told her. "Maybe I should get one too—I'll look into it."

We enjoyed a good laugh and finished our visit. When we said our goodbyes I promised to return, then I drove my mother home. I didn't tell either woman how I had secreted Annie Pearl's request away with me.

Already I knew I would get her a fur coat, even if I had to walk into Bergdorf's, put down my credit card, and pony up a thousand dollars I most certainly didn't have. I was delighted she asked me for something, happy to have such a hopeful mission. A few days later, I went back home to Manhattan with a sense of purpose and anticipation. I felt purpose because I truly wanted to thank her for the memories of my father she had given me. I felt anticipation because I knew how much she would love getting a package from me. I kept picturing the UPS man bringing the box up her porch steps, and how much she would squeal when she opened it and realized what it was and whom it was from.

It's that feeling of how much I wanted to say "Yes" to Annie Pearl, and how diligently I moved forward with that yes over the course of several months, that I look back on now. I think about searching out that fur for Annie Pearl every time I put off something my mother has requested of me. Even now there's an unfulfilled request: my mother asked for an enlargement of a family photo I've recently taken with my husband and son. The picture file is on the computer or on our family desk somewhere. I have yet to look for it or even ask my husband where it is. I've grown tired of her requesting. I've grown exhausted of the giving for holidays as well as for everyday appeals like the photo. She likes to make sure she gets her presents and when I call her on a holiday she will run down the list of what gifts and money she's received. When she recites such bounty I'm loathe to add to the pile of stuff.

I started my search for Annie Pearl's fur at work. I wrote for *People* magazine and it seemed to me as much as we reported on celebrities and their clothing, someone in the office would know how to buy a fur coat at a reasonable price. My inquiries paid off better than I expected: One of my colleagues told me the socialites of the Upper East Side often cast off their old furs to neighborhood thrift stores. I could probably find a nice one at a Goodwill for a couple hundred dollars or less. This information provided such relief—I dreaded the thought of entering door upon door of Fifth Avenue or Madison Avenue shops and sneaking peeks at price tags and having security guards eyeing me suspiciously. I could walk into a thrift store with no more bother than a Barnes & Noble. So began my process of locating such stores, calling them to ask if they had any fur coats in stock and if they did, going there to examine the furs in person.

What I write about my mother and my attitude toward fulfilling her requests or giving her gifts may make me seem cold, immature, or even ungrateful. I'm not afraid of those labels, but I want it known that I'm aware of them. And what comes next I tell not by way of excuse or explanation. This is just how it is for me, and my writing about it is still my coming to understand why I feel this way, and why I can't seem to hold for my mother the kind of forgiveness I cultivated—and still do—for my father. I began thinking about this last spring when I attended a writers retreat in Missouri and I stood beside a river discussing flaws with a friend who was also participating in the retreat. He asked if I had any flaws. I quietly noted my mother had called and left a voice mail a few days earlier and I had yet to respond.

I didn't know what to say to him after that because the sentence sounded so common. Many adult children avoid their mothers' messages—the whole concept is fodder for jokes in movies and television shows and has been for ages. But I know how unfunny my feelings are—how much anger and lack of compassion anchored my neglecting to call her back. I didn't see how I could explain it in the course of one conversation. It's even harder for someone who has met my mother to understand what I'm talking about. Most people find her so sweet and small (she was once four feet eleven but seems to be shrinking every year) and childlike—she will recite one of the many religious poems she's collected over the years: "I begin my day with Jesus . . ." at the drop of a hat. But she does this well because she wants approval, she wants to please—and it is exactly this characteristic that upsets me.

I soon discovered these socialites who gave away their furs were often tiny. Tom Wolfe's "social x-rays" from his novel *Bonfire of the Vanities* came to mind whenever I attempted to push my arms into coat sleeves that were too narrow. I'm not especially tall myself—just 5'5"—but my shoulders are broad, my arms muscular. I tried the furs on myself because I figured Annie Pearl and I were about the same size even if she had a bit more heft around the middle. If it could fit me, with room to spare, she could wear it comfortably. Whenever I walked into a store and saw several coats—mink, fox, sable, white, black, brown, striped—my heart would get pumped up with hope—certainly Annie Pearl's fur was among them. But then I'd get deflated, little by little, as each coat proved too small. I would go home to the West Side annoyed because I still didn't have the coat and because traveling any-where on the East Side of Manhattan, with its long crosstown blocks, crowded buses, and only one subway—the Lexington Ave-nue line—ate into my sense of quest every time I ventured there.

When I was growing up it often seemed as though my mother wasn't an adult, but an older child who had a bunch of younger ones placed in her care. My father confirmed this idea for us regu-larly and often told the story of how, when they were first mar-ried and lived with my mother's father, he came home from work to find the house dirty and my mother, who was then in her late twenties, out jumping rope in the street with some girls. And how he beat her and how necessary it was. But the memory that sticks with me most involves the time when our family was sitting in our tiny living room and my siblings and I were eating candy and watching television. I don't remember where we got this candy, but I do remember what my father said.

"You give your mother some of that candy. You know she's like a child—she's sitting there and she wants some but she's afraid to ask you for any."

My siblings and I looked at each other. What Daddy said sounded so strange that it seemed like a joke, at least that's what I thought. Still, one of us jumped up and gave the candy to her, and I think that was the beginning of my mother not being afraid to ask for anything because she knew we would have to give it. But for me the moment opened a window on what I already sus-pected: my mother was indeed a child masquerading as an adult. This explained why whenever I tried to talk to her or, to be hon-est, voice my complaints about the way our father treated us, she never reacted in the way I expected. Once, for instance, I told her how I felt like a slave because of the way he hit us and how he would take us out to farm fields to pick apples or collard greens that we had to sit and peel, or cut and freeze for hours on end. She told Daddy what I said and I had to endure his wrath, including months of having my words thrown back into my face. The betrayal I felt for my mother cut deep, but the more I saw her childlike aspects the more I understood her behavior—she had gone and tattled on me, just like a child wanting an adult's approval might have done.

I consider the months—and the search did take months—I spent looking for that fur coat and I wonder if I was seeking Annie Pearl's approval even as I sought the elusive piece of finery. But I doubt this because, really, if I wanted to please Annie Pearl all I needed to do was show up. And I did, visiting her on the same trips in which I saw my mother. Annie Pearl never mentioned the fur coat, never requested anything else of me. So I must admit I was the one who had my heart set on the fur for reasons I'm slowly beginning to excavate. And I'm coming to see my mother inextricably linked here.

When I was fouteen my sister-in-law used to drop off her little boys for us to watch while she and my brother worked. One day Marcus, who was just a baby then, cried inconsolably in my arms after his mother drove away. I stood rocking him, talking to him. I was so certain I could comfort him and even more certain that my mother could not. She was sitting on the couch saying, "Give him to me," and I was ignoring her. I saw no reason why I should give him to her—she who had never comforted anyone in her life—and I knew this too well remembering nights when I or one of my siblings timidly knocked at my parents' locked bedroom door because one of us had thrown up in the bed or all over the bathroom floor. Her voice would be high-pitched, almost like a falsetto, as she emerged to help but with tears in her eyes and the complaint on her lips, "I can't get any sleep for you kids!"

But that afternoon the crying had gone on for too long. Daddy, incensed by the noise, hit me with his open hand, right up side the head. His hand felt solid, my head even more so, like the connection of a brick against stone but with neither breaking. Many times my father had called me hardheaded, and suddenly I understood what that could mean. The blow was enough to stagger me but I managed to hold on to Marcus. Then I handed him over to my mother and left the room as tears brimmed over in my eyes. I refused to sob in front of them.

This memory itches. I feel it when I'm in a Bath & Body Works store trying to remember what was the last gift set I bought for my mother there and wondering if she would even notice if I gave her the same thing twice. My mother's birthday is in January, less than three weeks after Christmas. I don't know why I still haven't developed the habit of getting her both gifts, Christmas and birthday, while doing my holiday shopping. Around New Year's she begins her petition, reminding my siblings and me of her day coming up. She did this even after my father died the week before her birthday, but I was probably too crazed with grief to mind. In fact I felt fine about sending her gifts, requested and not, in the first years after he died. I would send her the extra handbags I'd acquired from frequenting sample sales as a fashion editor. I mailed magazines, puzzle books, and ribbon candy—her favorite. I felt sorry for her living by herself. I remember taking her home one night after visiting Annie Pearl and watching her climb the steps to the stone slab that was our porch and watching her unlock the door under the glow of the light my father had always set by a timer to come on at dusk. It made me sad to think of the empty house she entered. She looked so small and alone.

I can't tell you when giving gifts to my mother lost all meaning. Perhaps it dawned on me one evening while watching *A Charlie Brown Christmas* and hearing with new ears the letter that Sally, Charlie Brown's little sister, wanted to send to Santa. After noting how long her list will be she adds, "If it seems too complicated, make it easy on yourself. Just send money. How about tens and twenties?" It made sense to me. I've since mailed many checks for my mother's birthday and Mother's Day and Christmas. The feeling was the same—like I was throwing all these presents and clothes and money into a voracious black hole. But any piece of jewelry, stationery set, or bottles of lotion seemed to please her. As long as I sent something I would be off the hook until the next occasion when once again I'd buy a new item and toss it into the void.

The fur for Annie Pearl would not go into a void. I was determined it would have meaning for myself and for her. The quest itself, stuffed with love and possibilities, captured my imagination. Who in the world asks for a fur coat, and from a stranger no less? And the search, despite my crosstown travels to the East Side, was fun and interesting. I didn't worry about animal rights. I knew I would be sending the fur to a place where most people probably thought PETA was a pet shop at the Midway Mall. I wondered what kind of fur I would eventually find. Would it be mink? Frankly, I didn't think about the animals. I was probably still referencing my childhood, before I knew a mink was an animal, when it was always a coat and one that looked soft and impossibly light. Would Annie Pearl's fur be like that—a luxurious number like the ones I'd seen casually tossed to servants by laughing socialites in the glamorous films of the 1940s?

In 2002 my sister Theo left Michigan after earning her master's degree in library science and moved in with our mother. Theo was born fifteen days before my first birthday, making her my Irish twin, but we were as opposite as two sisters could be. I have light skin; she was dark. My hair is red; hers was black. I tend to be determined, proactive, and more prone to push my way through the world. She seemed to think that life just happened to her and was constantly perplexed over whether or not she could control anything. She was only supposed to stay in our childhood home temporarily, but Theo, perhaps because she was a daily witness to our mother's aging, came to feel she could never leave. She took a job as a student services coordinator at the local community college and, as arthritis and various health issues affected our mother's physique and mobility, Theo acquired the role of caregiver.

My sister also loved to cook, and her weight ballooned to well over 200 pounds while she lived with and maintained our mother. I'm not privy to how Theo lived her life or how these things came to happen to her, but for the purposes of my story you need to know this. My sister had bariatric surgery in 2004 and she lost a lot of weight. In photos from our 2005 family reunion she smiles and looks healthy. She and I and our three other sisters are wearing matching purple T-shirts and standing in a row behind our seated mother. A few years later she began to gain weight again and suffer complications of the procedure. In March 2011, I visited and was shocked to find Theo bloated and unwell. I begged her to fight for her life as she made comments about seeing our ancestors in her dreams and how we should get pink carnations for her funeral. But at the same time she made me believe she would try to get better and we began an ongoing communication that made it seem like she was doing so. We had conference calls with our siblings to schedule regular "respite time" when one of us or a home care aid would look after Mom so Theo could focus on herself. She arranged visits with her doctors and would call me late at night to talk about her treatment—she said she needed surgery for scar tissue in her abdomen—and the book about caregiving that she wanted to write someday. As much as I cherish the memory of these calls I'm not sure she had been telling me the whole truth. I think she was far sicker for far longer than she let on to any of us. That June she checked into a hospital and was diagnosed with a severe pancreatic infection. She died within days.

The morning we got the call that Theo had passed away, my husband asked me, "What's going to happen when your mother finds out?"

I shook my head. "She'll only want to know who's going to take care of her now."

"Really? But her daughter is dead. And they lived together for years."

"Yes, but that's just how my mom's brain works."

When I traveled to my oldest brother's home to prepare for the funeral I had to ask the question. Maybe I was hoping for a different answer.

"How did Mom take it when you told her Theo was gone?"

I remember his voice, soft and heavy with disbelief. "She just looked at me and asked, 'Who's going to take care of me now?' She hasn't cried or anything."

He worried that this was some function of our mother's age, that her grief was so deep it had done something to her mind.

He even took her to a psychologist to have her checked. "The doctor said she's unable to process emotion like everyone else does," my brother explained. "It's like she's in a persistent child-like state."

He said this as though it were a new development. My brother was in shock, but I didn't understand how he didn't know this his whole life—she'd been his mother for nine years longer than she'd been mine.

As much as I have known who and what she is, a part of me thinks my mother is a sly child sitting in the back of the school bus, watching the bus driver's rearview mirror so she can jump up and down or move seats when she knows the driver isn't watching. Such a child knows better. I've often wondered if my mother does too and makes a conscious decision not to be an adult. I wanted her to be an adult. I wanted her to be the mother my sister had sorely needed.

I have a confession to make here. I wasn't always diligent in my quest for the fur coat. Life intervened—projects at work, vacations, parties, or the occasional bad cold did the usual number on my priorities, pushing down what once lived on the top of my to-do list. Weeks, even months would pass before subtle reminders nudged me, such as the death of an elderly celebrity like Ella Fitzgerald, or I would find myself sitting across from an Annie Pearl doppelganger on the subway. At these times I worried Annie Pearl would disintegrate quickly as my father had done. He died within three weeks of the doctor's first sighting the spots on my father's lungs. But despite the suddenness of his death, I was quite aware that I held no sense of deeds left undone where my father and I were concerned, save for a wish I once had to buy him a new car. The important things—time well spent with him, forgiveness felt in my heart and delivered, every phone call returned—had been completed. I recognized and appreciated the freedom of this completion—no loose ends dangling, every promise—especially the self-inflicted ones—fulfilled. I wanted the same for my story with Annie Pearl.

A few days before Theo's funeral I visited my mother in the little house Theo had bought for them just a couple of years earlier. The home sat a block from Lakeview Park on a street whose walker/wheelchair friendly sidewalks led to the beach. Theo did the landscaping herself and instead of mulch she had put down sparkling pink stone gravel in the beds around her flowers. I picked up one of the stones and put it in my pocket as I walked into the house. My mother sat watching *Family Feud* in the massage recliner Theo had procured for her with Medicaid funding. Her walker was positioned nearby as well as a TV tray that held her puzzle books, the TV remote, and, I saw, the newspaper.

"Mom, isn't this the paper with Theo's obituary?"

She nodded as I picked it up and folded the pages open to the photo of my sister's face—her curly dark hair shining, her bright smile glowing. I placed the paper on the table so my mother could see it. A few minutes later she turned it over and covered it with a department store circular.

At the funeral, in between talking to people who knelt or bent over her to deliver their condolences, my mother would motion me to come over and tell me which of the many floral arrangements she wanted to take home. She didn't want the flowers, she said, only the houseplants, which would last longer.

Whatever forgiveness I had managed for my mother—and I like to think I had scraped together a little—about the way we were brought up, about her inability to fight for us or protect us, all came undone with Theo's death. I believed the same void into which I had thrown a multitude of gifts had at last taken a significant one: it swallowed Theo whole. I still wrestle, shamefully, with resentment for my mother because of this. For all my father's violence and bombast, I know he would have been devastated at the death of one of his children. He would have cried—and I had seen my father cry. He would have sat on the side of his bed and not come out for hours, as he had done when his fraternal twin, Virgil, died when I was eight. Then there was the time when one of my younger sisters was sick and my mother had been slow to take her temperature. My father came home from work and we all went to the emergency room where we found out that my sister had a dangerously high fever. I remember how mad he was at my mother, saying, "You could have messed around here and lost that child." I used to wonder what that meant. Lose how? And why was he so worried about it? I thought of this again when Theo died—we'd lost that child. But my mother, no matter how much she may have really felt the loss, could never make it seem like she cared.

One day in an Upper East Side thrift store, I slipped on a long silver gray fox fur that was perfectly too large in all the right places. I cupped the price tag hanging from the right cuff in both my hands. Seventy-five dollars, it read. I thought my heart would split with glee as I stood in front of a full-length mirror examining the fur from all sides. I appreciated the coat's lightness and warmth even though I could never wear such a thing—but then in that moment I wasn't myself. I was Annie Pearl and Louise Jefferson both at the same time.

I remember the excitement of getting a shipping box big enough to fit the coat. As I packed the fur carefully in a garment bag surrounded by tissue paper, I kept picturing Annie Pearl opening the box, imagining how ecstatic she would be to see the coat. It didn't even matter to me that I wouldn't be there to witness this myself.

But these days I find that vision blends with another, one of my mother opening just such a box. I was home from college, home for Christmas, and one of my younger sisters had informed me that the current drama in the house was our mother's need for a new winter coat and our father's refusal to buy her one. My sister and I immediately went to the Hills department store where we rummaged through racks until we found a coat we thought our mother would like. It was a cornflower blue parka with a hood and big front pockets. We got a gift box for it and wrapped it in secret. Then, to throw our mother off track because she was always nosy about what she was being given for Christmas, I put my sister's name on the box before putting it under the tree.

That Christmas morning after most of the packages had been opened, I handed the big box to her. My siblings and I gathered around. When she pulled out the coat she held it up to the light then hugged it to her, "Oh my goodness! It's so pretty!" And I saw—I think—I'm certain, I think—I saw a few tears fall from the corner of her right eye. My father sat in his chair and sulked. When I thought about it later I know he probably felt humiliated—most likely he didn't buy her a coat because he couldn't afford to, not because he didn't want to. But whenever I think of that Christmas his hurt is secondary. I wonder about my mother's reaction, and how her pleasure was so real. I got to experience all the elements that make gift giving enjoyable: the recipient's surprise combined with my own satisfaction from fulfilling a wish or a need, and the gift being the right vessel of that fulfillment.

Years later I packed Annie Pearl's box hoping for the same satisfaction.

After I mailed the coat I half expected my mother, when she saw Annie Pearl's fur, to request one for her but instead she crocheted a gray beret for Annie Pearl to match the coat. My older brother saw the debut of this finery when Annie Pearl wore the fur and her hat to church. "You should have seen her strutting down that aisle!" he said, but I didn't need to. I already felt complete, at least complete with Annie Pearl.

Now Annie Pearl is long gone. My mother, at the time of this writing, is eighty-one years old. As I sit here there is a voicemail from her on my cellphone that has gone unanswered for two days. I wait and I think and I wonder: will I have any regret about the calls unreturned, the photos unsent, when my mother passes on?

THE WORLD DON'T TURN THAT WAY FOR ME, DADDY

I. ONE DAY

My father's letter lies dormant in the bottom of my jewelry box—dormant like Tolkien's ring of power threatening to waken at any moment and bring ruin to a lifetime of carefully forged love and forgiveness. And lately, like Tolkien's ring, I think I hear it whispering to me, and I know I am craving the sound of my father's voice even if it is filled with scolding.

This letter, berating me for a poor report card I received in my junior year of college, has been shoved angrily in the bottom of a backpack, hidden in piles of paper, re-discovered again and again in de-cluttering frenzies—but it has not been re-read. My heart hurts even to think of it and yet, for the first time in some twenty-five years, I want to open it once more.

Maybe it was the photo of our father that my sister Jeanette e-mailed to me this summer on my forty-sixth birthday. He is standing next to the bronze-colored fifteen-passenger monstrosity once known as the Scottmobile. I had been forced to drive this extended van as a teenager, becoming the family chauffeur to both parents and siblings when, unknown to me, my father's eyes developed cataracts and he was having trouble seeing. My sister sent the picture because she said Daddy would be tickled to know I was learning to drive a school bus. In the photo my father looms broad and large, yet there is something shrunken about him as well. His head seems too small for his body and the looseness of his pants tells me of the shrunken limbs beneath the polyester fabric. I realize this picture must have been taken a year or two before he died. If I look closely I see the rust spots on the van, bubbling up underneath the paint.

My father looks so frail and vulnerable. I know he loved me and perhaps it is the combination of that thought and the photograph that make me hunger for his voice again. Perhaps I am in need of that unconditional, if unruly and bombastic, love. Since my father could neither read nor write this letter was, as all his letters were, dictated to my mother and written in her careful penmanship on lined notebook paper. I remember this process as a child. "Say that back to me" and my mother would read the writing to show she had gotten the words exactly right for notes like one he might send to borrow money from a friend: "If you will send me $40 I will pay you back $50 on the third of the month when I get my Social Security check. You know I am good for it."

Perhaps my desire to read the letter is about some need to test what I've taught my own son: that when you love you can get hurt. However, the hurt goes away. The love remains. This is the thought that makes the most sense to me because it has been one of the most profound experiences of my life—to have been hurt by a loved one and having that feeling of being tight and curled up like my heart would live forever encased in a bomb shelter to keep it from being wounded again. But then I would emerge, blinking in the dazzling light and realizing, though the muscles felt stretched and stressed, that I still loved—and loved the person who had hurt me no less. I always felt so much stronger afterward. How strong would I be if I could endure such stress from the words of my long-dead father?

The work I've done I believe to be meticulous. And I did it without a therapist. All of the answers are within us—it's just a matter of pouring out the pieces and looking honestly at each one, peeling off the emotion, lies, and, last of all, the story I've told myself about all those pieces just so I could endure them. For instance, I had always told myself, when I lived at home, that my father didn't love me. If so he wouldn't have hit me the many times that he did; he wouldn't say such horrible things to me, calling me a yellow-skinned bastard. Why did he say that when I so obviously had the rusty hair color that ran like a burning river throughout his side of the family line? It was the things he said that have stayed with me, that hurt the most. I do worry about remembering the sting of the electric cord on my legs and arms. I remember how heavy his hand felt as it landed across my face. The sting and red welts of the electric cord, though, disappeared after awhile. But his words? They lasted longer—hence my fear of the letter. And yet there were the pieces I had chosen to ignore because they didn't seem to fit the picture—times when he tried to console me when I was inconsolable, like when John Lennon died and I cried for days and wore black to school. To look back on it now I see so much of it was probably fueled by puberty and an adolescent's sense of drama. But I think he could tell my heart truly hurt and because mine did, his heart hurt as well. He drove me to a department store and bought me a mirror etched with an image of the Beatles from their *Rubber Soul* album for $14.99, an extravagant amount for our family, to ease my fourteen-year-old's grief. I still have it, this relic of my father's love. I've packed it carefully each time I've moved. After all these years it remains unbroken.

I thought I had examined so carefully all my relics and stories and now I worry this letter will show me a missing piece—a gaping canyon that I don't have the means to fill. What would I do then?

But I feel the inevitability of this letter—that I must open it because this aspect of my father wants very much to manifest itself in my current novel. I always said I put the good parts of my father in my first novel. I thought that was all there would be to it. I once read something that said when a father dies you can't, for the life of you, remember one bad thing about him. I've been content to fall into this comfortable fog of forgetfulness. It surprises me now to think about how much I once feared him—and still do. Now I see the bad parts of him turning up: I created a mother character who plays her daughters against each other, who sees worth in terms of money and skin tone. This character talks but rarely listens, but the daughters love her anyway. Is that possible?

Perhaps this is the answer—not that I am in need of a vast, certain, unconditional love. It is a need, maybe even desperation to know that I can love unconditionally. And reading this letter would be the ultimate test—it will measure all I have accumulated and learned and absorbed about love. It will tell me how strong my heart really is, so I can be confident in that strength when it is called upon to be resilient in the face of a challenge—I can love unconditionally my husband, my son, my most cherished friends in the moments when it may be hardest to do so.

But why the need to test myself now?

If I can once again feel the shackles of fearing my father, I know I will be that much lighter when I'm assured I am really free of them. Maybe I'm seeking the simple joy I had in college when I was happy just to walk down the street—I would run an errand for a classmate who was too lazy to go out for a bottle of soda—because it made me giddy to know for a fact the Scottmobile would not come rumbling up behind me.

Is it coming now? Let me turn and address it again.

II. ANOTHER DAY

My friend Maria suggests I take the letter and read it out in the woods or an open field, somewhere safe where I can kick and scream and cry at will. I think I would feel like Harry Potter going out in the woods with my own horcrux, this living piece of my father's soul that I know carries a dozen mirror images of what my heart truly looks like. What will I see? I worry I will dive into this pond and images and memories of the dead will snatch at me and hold me down, never to resurface.

Maria is right, I know. If I read the letter where I feel safe, perhaps in a place very familiar to me, I will stay where I am. The letter will have a harder time pulling me out of myself, back to my twenty-year-old mind that didn't have the protection of hindsight and understanding that I have today. When my father had a thought he used to say, "My mind came to me today and told me. . . ." I will have to remember that—remember to keep my wits about me so my forty-six-year-old mind can be at the ready to say what I most need to hear when the time comes.

I have made such preparations before, but for my heart and not my mind. In the pre-Facebook world I have had to consciously make space for loved ones separated from me by distance and by life. In doing this, letters and photos are precious tools. I re-read e-mails and letters from people like my college classmates. I keep on my walls and shelves photos of people I wished lived down the street. I feed on these items so I can believe the love in either direction doesn't disappear for lack of words or physical connection. This is what one has to do to endure the pain of missing them, otherwise the pain will grow instead of diminish. Simone Weil once said, "For when two beings who are not friends are near each other there is no meeting, and when friends are far apart there is no separation." If I were sitting near my father today would there be any meeting? The choice, I think, is up to me. I'm thinking of the story about the two dogs we all have within us: one is loving and positive, the other is ferocious and negative. Which one wins? The one you feed the most. So I make the space and feed the light. I've done that with my father in the past. Can I do it again?

The first time this light blew full into being was when my father died. I felt grief but then there was something else. I felt wild like I could do anything and no one—at least no one I really cared about—could say a thing to me. I feared nothing and no one and I wanted to run down the street screaming this freedom. My world was destroyed and rebuilt in a single day and my whole being rung with this newborn energy. My grief was fierce and it pushed me to take hold of my life in a way that was entirely new to me. I didn't care about anything other than how to do it.

Suddenly I didn't have time for niceties or half-truths. When my father died, Darryl and I had been in this place of kind of seeing each other again after having been engaged and then not engaged when he called it off. At that point we had been in a relationship, mostly long distance, for four years. When my father died and this craziness took hold of me, I told Darryl that I loved him, but I didn't have time for whatever was happening in our relationship. I had to go take on the world, and he could either come with me or not. I really didn't care anymore. He decided he wanted to, yes, but the point I want to make is how when a parent dies, no one talks about having this kind of feeling. At least I'd never heard of it before. Most people speak of pain and loss and that's all. The only person I know who has touched on this other feeling, this wild openness, was the playwright August Wilson, speaking through the character of Memphis in *Two Trains Running*. Memphis says this on how he felt when he'd heard of the death of his mother: "I cried till the tears all run down in my ears. Got up and went out the door and everything looked different. Everything had changed. I felt like I had been cut loose. All them years something had a hold of me and I didn't know it. I didn't find out till it cut me loose. I walked out the door and everything had different colors to it. I felt great. I didn't owe nobody nothing. The last person I owed anything to was gone."

Am I really cut loose? Or does something still have a hold of me now?

III. TODAY

I've decided the safest place to read the letter is sitting on one of the swings of my son's playground set. The set is mounted in a bed of mulch at the edge of the woods that climb a hill behind our house. If the reading goes badly I can run up into the forest where I can kick and scream to my heart's content.

I open the jewelry box and remove the top tray containing items such as my silver bracelet engraved with a Rilke quote, fake diamond-studded earrings, and a prayer bead necklace. I don't see the letter at first—it's buried under a cashmere satchel containing a large necklace made with pieces of orange glass. I have truly hidden it, but then there it is: two pages of college-ruled notebook paper yellowed with time, written through on both sides—four pages in all. It seems shorter than I remembered. Before whenever I thought of it in the box I saw voluminous pages multiplying until the letter threatened to raise the box's lid and break its hinges. I see the date on the top of the first page and recognize my mother's handwriting: 1–27–87. Already I feel something in my abdomen hardening. I take a deep breath.

I have to clear away spider webs before I can properly sit on the blue plastic swing. I keep my feet planted firmly as I move myself back and forth, just a gentle rocking to soothe myself before the words to come. The neighborhood is quiet after a morning of school buses rumbling through, first the high school and middle school run, then the intermediate school, and then the elementary that took my son with it. I do feel safe in this sort of marble with a rain-washed blue sky above me and the yellowing tree leaves all around me, and damp brown mulch beneath me. This is my home, I tell myself. I am fine. I've done nothing wrong. I unfold the letter and read.

Hi Sophfronia,

    Just a few lines from home to give you a little advise and also to let you know that we are both (Mom + Dad) are praying for you.

    Sophfronia this is your daddy speaking to you. You are the cause of this your own self as you have your mind on men to much when you should be thinking of your own self. You have your mind on men over seas and men in Connecticut when you should have your mind on your studying. The reason why I am telling you this Sophfronia you know that you know Dr. Eren, you also know Dr. Lynk that operated on my eyes and Dr. Miclat my heart specialist. When you go to these doctors if the doctors are busy, their wives wait on you because they are doctors also. This is the kind of man that you should deal with.

Instead of going to New Mexico you should have found a doctor there to help you and work with you so that it would not be so hard for you.

You make a pattern out of that sweater that you sent me with Harvard on it. I can put that sweater on and go up town and I can't count the white people shaking my hand and asking me how am I doing because I have Harvard on that sweatshirt.

Just like Attorney Gordon said it is hard in college and you have to study hard to make the grade. You can not be running after no man. . . .

Sophfronia if you were a doctor, you could not wait on your patient with your mind on a man. I could not explain this to you if I did not know what I was talking about. If I didn't I would lie to you.

On the 8th of May in 1953 my 1st wife run off and left me. I was working for U.S. Steel. The superintendent come out on the job and asked me Scott where is that woman gone to and I told him that she was gone St. Louis. He said I am giving you one hundred dollars to go get the woman and bring her back to me as I don't want to see you lose your mind. I went to St. Louis but I didn't find the woman. When she died they would not let me go to her funeral and U.S. Steel pays me when I go to a funeral.

You have got to deal with people that want to be a doctor like you and not deal with the wrong kind of people. . . .

Sophfronia don't you know that those people in that college is watching you.

If you go the right way them people will help you.

You have been up there long enough to run that college up there for as smart as you were here.

That college is too hard for you to have 2 things on your mind and that is what is the matter with you.

Sophfronia I am your dad and I am suppose to tell you right from wrong. Cut out some of your pleasure things and take more time to study.

I got on my knees and prayed to God about you last night and he led me to write you and tell you this.

Look Sophfronia don't get me wrong. You are a grown woman now and I can say what I want to but you are going to do like you want.

You look I try to help you all that I can when I could be flying all over the world just like other old people.

You have a long way to go up the road and you had better watch yourself. Closing for now. Write me when you get this letter. From Mom + Dad

At first I shake my head and then calmness comes over me. My arms feel weak, like I've been holding them up over my head for a long time, waiting for a blow that never came. I can put them down now. I lean forward in the swing and it feels as though I am sitting next to my father in his battered, patched recliner, the one he always sat in. I am sitting as I always did when I came home to visit, listening to him, responding with the usual, "Yes, sir." I'm leaning forward as I'd done before. Back then I was considering the answer to a question he had asked me many, many, years ago: "Why do you have to go away to school? Why can't you find a man to take care of you?"

I had wanted to rail at him then, to scream, "Haven't you noticed I've barely had a boy look my way let alone date me? Wasn't that why you put a chain link fence, five feet high, all around our house? What a silly question! Don't you know I have to get out of this house or die?"

Instead I sat leaned forward, my elbows on my knees. I looked into his face and said, "The world don't turn that way for me, Daddy."

I explained about wanting to be able to take care of myself, about how this was the only way I could become a doctor. (I didn't talk about writing because I didn't know then it could be a vocation.) I don't recall if he said anything afterward. Perhaps he nodded. Perhaps he was already trying to figure out how to ensure my safety at a distance of 500 miles. Perhaps he was hurting and didn't know how to let me go. But this memory eases the sting of the letter. This memory told me what I had forgotten:

1) My father was willing to listen and learn.

2) I could talk to him, especially in moments like this when he made an opening available.

Years ago I had not recognized it, but in reading the letter now I could see here was such a moment. Maybe he recognized this too, and that's why he had sent words back to me in the form of this letter. He had even asked for a response and I don't think I ever sent one. I guess I can do that now.

First of all, I have to acknowledge the love and concern in this letter: he didn't call me any names. In fact, he said I was a grown woman and could do what I wanted. He was obviously worried about what that was. I will also say that he was right: my mind was cleaved in two, and had been for most of my college career. But he had the wrong two things. It had nothing to do with men. Yes, I went to New Mexico, but that was over the summer, after freshman year, not during the school year. My friend who lived in Connecticut was working at the Santa Fe Opera house that summer and I got to learn about the desert and music and live performance under a black star-filled sky. But that friend was gay. I never had a boyfriend in college.

I would explain to my father that the other thing pulling for my attention then was writing. I would have asked him to notice that the only poor grades I had were science grades. But then I remind myself that he couldn't read, perhaps that had added to my frustration all those years ago. How could I explain to him how resentful I felt every time I purchased a biology textbook four inches thick when what I really wanted to be reading was George Eliot's *Daniel Deronda*? He wouldn't have known that the books I asked him to send me from the Lorain Public Library were poetry books: Shelley and Keats and Lord Byron. He was, in three short years, already so invested in the idea of my becoming a doctor that it would have been meaningless to tell him of the paper I had written about Shelley—a paper I still have to this day—that received an A+ and a note from my teacher saying I obviously understood the romantics very well. I was good at that study, really good. But I was essentially doing a double workload, sneaking in English and writing classes in addition to neurobiology and organic chemistry. I didn't want to do it anymore. Would he have understood if I had told him beforehand that I was in the process of switching majors?

Maybe I could have written to him and said: *Daddy, I am a writer. I can tell stories. And you know what? I get it from you. You've been telling me stories my whole life, just like the story of your first wife leaving you. Please don't worry. I'm staying in school, I'm switching majors, and I will study English instead. I won't even have to add on semesters because I've done so many of the requirements already. I will still have a job and be able to take care of myself when I graduate. Thank you for praying for me.*

I didn't know enough to tell him this when he sent me the letter. But that's what I did. I ended up going to *Time* magazine. And I know he was proud of me because when those same people who shook his hand when he wore his Harvard sweatshirt came up to him again he would show them my name in the magazine, copies of which he always kept in the van. In fact my first and last name, the same as his mother's, were the only words he could decipher on the page.

I wish my father could have known me better. That is the sadness, the regret I feel as I sit on the swing. It is indeed a gaping canyon that I can never cross. But I am not angry; I am not fearful or mournful or paralyzed in a childlike state. Actually I am thinking about a little girl named Alex Deford. I know of her because the noted sportswriter Frank Deford wrote *Alex, the Life of a Child,* a memoir about his daughter who died in 1980 of cystic fibrosis at the age of eight. The book was made into a TV movie and I viewed it both when I was in high school and at college. There were parts in the film where Alex used to say to him, "Oh my Daddy, my little Daddy!" and she would shake her head or put her hands on his face and laugh. Every time she did, it broke my heart. I sat on the verge of tears not knowing why. I think I understand it now. Some part of me knew then that there would always be this limitation, where I would always have knowledge my father would not or could not have. That for all his bigness there would be this part that would always remain small. It would require my patience and, yes, my unconditional love. I can only hold this letter in my hands and think, "Oh my Daddy, my little Daddy." And with this thought I am free.

CALLING ME BY MY NAME

"Sophfronia. I've never heard that name before. It's so pretty. How did your mother come up with it?"

That's when it begins. My chin descends like a stone dropping into the depths of a lake until my eyes reach a level where I think my inquirer will be able to sense what I'm about to say is significant. "My father . . ." I say the second word slowly; I can feel my tongue darting into the second syllable just under my two front teeth. And just in case there's any chance the person I'm addressing may miss the point, I nod slightly with a little bounce of the chin ". . . named me after his mother."

I may have done this for years, but I've only recently caught myself doing it, perhaps because there have been so many more chances to do so. I'm currently studying for my master's in creative writing, so I'm meeting new people who happen to be curious artists, like myself, who want to know the origins of things. It startles me how I respond in this manner when I get this particular question. I don't place such gravity in answering other questions about my name: *What nationality is it? Have you met anyone else with that name? How do you spell that? Can I call you Sophie?* Pride nudges me a bit, keeping me from allowing this notion to pass uncorrected. My father, dead now for over twenty years, named me. Not every child can say that. My four younger sisters definitely cannot. I find something grounding in the thought that whatever came later, as I grew older and our family grew larger, there was a moment in my life when I had Daddy's singular, shining focus. And this attention didn't come because I had not washed the dishes or I had burned a pot of greens or because I was hiding in the bathroom reading a book or any number of reasons he later saw fit to give me a whipping. In the moment he named me there would have been no booming voice pounding out obscenities, no red welts rising on my arms, and no fervent wishes that some kind soul would show up and offer to take me to boarding school, preferably in England, where I could fashion myself like Jane Eyre, trying to understand forgiveness and determination, all the while nursing a stale bitterness in my heart over how I had been treated. No, this focus was a loving one that manifested in an apple, its skin magically curling in spirals as Daddy peeled it for me, or the warmer version of his voice singing Muddy Waters songs while he tightened the bolts of the training wheels on my bike. Now my name brings me back to the moment of infancy, when I had done nothing but come into the world and my father, holding me close in his massive, brown steelworker's hands, poured into my tiny vessel of possibility the essence of what I would become: Sophfronia. This in turn conjures the larger hands I've always sensed upholding me, and the loving presence I've come to know as Creator Spirit affirming my name because I'd received a tremendous gift from my father but still in my childlike wonder needed to ask, "Is this really mine? Can I keep it?" And the presence in my heart responded, "Yes."

I know what pride feels like—it puffs me up like a bright sail full of wind—and it comes most often when my son says "Thank you" to a waitress or shares toys with his cousins or any of the many small actions parents tend to think are miracles. If my behavior were simply a matter of pride, then I would probably be doing more chest lifting and less chin lowering. This is more like I'm a toddler holding tight to a beloved bear because I think someone might take it away. As I sit with this child version of my heart and consider her insistence and determination, I begin to understand that I hold on to not just this particular detail, but to all aspects of my name, and I do so for a reason—because letter by letter, syllable by syllable, my name forms my connection to source. It's also a kind of shield that protects me and, on its glowing, reflective surface, shows me who I am.

I like considering the circumstances—what my father might have been thinking when he named me. He must have been seizing an opportunity. His mother, whose name I've seen noted on his birth certificate as "Sophronia Scott"—minus the "f" my name has—and "maiden name: Smith," died when he was about ten or twelve. And though he had nine siblings who spawned a vast multitude of grandchildren, none of these babies (a lot of whom were adults by the time I was born) had been named Sophfronia. So there I was, the third of my father's children but the first girl, and I received the name. I wonder how that conversation went, if there was indeed a conversation and not a proclamation. I've tried to mine my mother for the golden details with no luck. She loves to talk, but she is not the storyteller he was. Her answers, mundane to me, were simple truth for her: "That's just what he wanted to name you" or "He named you after his mama." But then when he was alive he had responded likewise. My parents didn't understand how I craved scene and detail, or that baby naming could take on dramatic proportions. So I don't know if my mother questioned the spelling of my name or if anyone helped her fill out the birth certificate—my father never learned to read. Though he could recognize my name in print when I earned my first bylines in *Time* magazine, where I worked after college, I doubt he could have ever spelled it. Most likely it was my mother who was responsible for the unnecessary "f" that perturbs readers and baffles spellers. "It's like wearing a belt and suspenders at the same time," I once told *Time*'s editor. My colleagues were impressed with how I had made him laugh.

This "f" goes missing on a regular basis. Even friends who know how to spell my name have misspelled it, as though their brains were on autocorrect long before autocorrect existed. I don't blame them. All other references to my name are "f"-less and even in the original Greek, which has no "f" in its alphabet, the spelling might be considered, perhaps, inaccurate. After my first day in first grade (my first experience in the education system) I went home and told my mother I sat at another girl's desk whose name was Sophronia, without an "f." She must have moved on to the next grade and I got her name tag on my desk because it was so close to my own. My mother told the teacher, Mrs. Kos, and my "f" appeared immediately. Mrs. Kos wanted to know why I hadn't asked her myself to fix it, but that was the way my brain worked in first grade. What I didn't understand I explained to myself by making up stories.

Today when I detect the absence of "f" I ask to have it corrected or I quietly take a pen and fix the errant name tag handed to me at events. One would think I would have grown tired of doing so and allowed my name to passively change, but I hold onto that "f" like a shepherd to his crook, as if I would be unidentifiable without it. My name looks flat and bereft when the "f" isn't there.

When I was in high school Miss Darcy, my Latin teacher, gave me something I never expected my name to have: a definition. She favored the habit of calling all her students by Latin names mirroring as closely as possible the meaning of their own. She sat on top of her desk, legs crossed, her head dipped into the pages of a huge etymological dictionary so that only her long frizzy brown curls stuck out from the sides like wings. When she emerged she pointed her long, double-jointed index finger at me until it nearly bent over backward. "You," she announced slowly with a proud, wide grin, "are Mens Sana. Of sound mind!" She broke it down and it seemed so simple, as though I should have always known it: the "soph" part meant "wisdom," the "fronia" or "phronius" translated as "the mind."

I absorbed this with wonder. Ever since I started school my teachers and classmates had called me "smart." As a first grader I barely knew what that meant, but it seemed to be a good thing because the librarian would allow me to check out books from the older kids' side of the room, and my parents liked showing off to their friends the approving comments Mrs. Kos wrote in

my report card. I wanted to keep reading and doing well in my
schoolwork so people would continue to think I was smart. But
then, to learn my name stood for a wise mind—it was like learning "smart" was who I was supposed to be all along. It didn't have
to depend on someone's say so. Suddenly my name had shape. It
felt like one of those magnificent Audrey Hepburn hats from *My
Fair Lady* had been placed upon my head. At first it seemed a
little too big, a little unwieldy, but I was determined to wear it.
I felt small but I recalled the loving presence, Creator Spirit, and
how it seemed to be around me, inside of me, saying my name
and affirming again, "Yes, this is yours." Whenever it was my turn
to write on the board and Miss Darcy would say, "Mens Sana will
be our amanuensis," I would walk to the board and hold my head
up under this new hat.

Since then I have gone from being totally empty of my name's
background to being filled to overflowing with its history and etymology, all of which I will cheerfully pour out to an inquisitor.
When asked how it ended up in my family, I point to the history
of American plantation owners calling their slaves ancient Greek
names such as Priam, Brutus, Althea, or Penelope. In another conversation I might explain how the name Sophronia and its various
forms, including Sofronia, Safronia, and Saphronia, was popular in the South at the turn of the century, and how my name-
sake grandmother had hailed from Mississippi. In fact a Google
search today will usually turn up several obituaries for elderly
Sophronias who have recently expired in Tennessee, Georgia,
or Alabama. Ancient records report that a man named Sophronius Tigellinus was a favorite of the emperor Nero as well as his
accomplice in the burning of Rome. A few years ago I learned of
a Pitt women's basketball player named Sophronia Sallard, and I
admit I once tuned into a television broadcast of the team's game
just so I could hear the announcer pronounce her name.

The playwright Lillian Hellman refers to her family maid
Sophronia as her "one certain love" who taught her righteous
anger. The playwright George Bernard Shaw had a sister named
Sophronia. Her name shows up in his plays: "We're off to visit

Aunt Sophronia." Sophronia shows up as a character in a few places I know of including the novels *The Life and Times of Captain N* by Douglas Glover, and *Personal Effects Dark Art* by J. C. Hutchins. The author of this last I met when he was a summer intern at *People* magazine. He found me on Twitter years later to proudly report he'd named a character after me (without the "f"). However, all of the Sophronias I've come across in literature are peripheral, not major characters. Writers tend to use the name to add dimension, not action, to their minor players.

In my sophomore year at Harvard, I took a class in the Crusades. In my reading I found a reference to a saint named Sophronius who died in 638 AD. Of course this piqued my interest, and I questioned the professor about it one afternoon. "Ah yes," she said, as though I had reminded her of something. "I noticed your name on the student roster and thought it was very curious. It is an old name, and it's not used much anymore."

She went on to explain that the "wisdom" and "sound mind" definitions of my name did not pertain to general knowledge, but a very specific one. "It's about knowing God," she said. "People over the years became uncomfortable with that idea, the concept of being close to God, of being able to know God in this way. So the name fell out of favor." I didn't know what she was talking about and, to be honest, I still don't. The Bible is stuffed with direct interactions with God and no one, to my knowledge, seems to take issue with that aspect of it. I have never seen any other reference to this idea of my professor's, not even in the vast ocean of information available on the worldwide web. I should have asked her to be more specific, to give me more background, more etymology.

I didn't, though, because in that moment I was silent and completely occupied with another line of thought involving the mysterious loving presence I'd always felt around me. I used to think I could see it in the rays of the sun filtered through clouds and I could talk to it when I played alone and searched for wild strawberries in the weedy fields near my parents' house. When I got older and came to understand faith, I knew I had been praying, not just talking, and the presence on the receiving end was most likely God. But I didn't know how to practice or explore this faith. Though my maternal grandfather had been a Baptist minister and my mother, as a teenager, taught Sunday school, my parents didn't take us to church. Still I developed with the presence a relationship mirroring that of a physical parent, sometimes in the most earth-bound, human ways. As a teenager, for instance, I would pray for my basketball team to win and when we didn't, I would pitch a little hissy fit with God that basically amounted to my trying to ignore His presence and not pray.

Thinking on it now, I probably needed to do this because there was no way I would have gotten away with a fit of any kind in front of Daddy. But the silent treatment, I learned, doesn't work with the divine—we always fell back into conversation, even a deeper one than where we left off. Sometimes I felt I should be in a church worshipping formally if only because I did feel this presence, I knew it was real, and I worried that if I didn't go to church I might waste the connection, like a talent uncultivated. I did try attending services of different denominations, both while I was in college and at different times afterward, but I couldn't find a place that seemed in alignment with my experience of this presence. However, what my professor told me that day awakened a hope in my heart that said I need not worry—it was like a promise that I would one day understand this presence more. Simultaneously I felt comfort and confusion. Part of me wanted to indulge in a childlike satisfaction: I knew a secret no one else on the playground knew. But the other part of me wondered again about this gift and whether I could ever truly understand it. I carry this conversation with me still, like a dark lantern waiting to be lit.

❦

I like Nina Simone's song "Four Women" because it seems to appreciate that a name like Sophfronia is not just a name but also a story, a history even, in and of itself. She used the spelling of my name that evokes the color yellow, "Saffronia," and the lyric makes it evident why she did so:

My skin is yellow . . .
Between two worlds
I do belong . . .

I know Saffronia does not have the same meaning or the same spelling as my name, but I do have the look known in the African-American community as "high yella, red-boned." My grandmother, if the stories are true, had similar features. That "between two worlds" lyric speaks to me because to look at me I would seem to fit everywhere and nowhere. When people meet me, for some of them, the question is there: *"What are you?"* They ask it directly or they ask it silently in the way their eyes sweep over my kinky reddish-brown hair, dark eyes, skin neither dark nor white, and the constellation of freckles that decorate my face. I surprise more than a few when I say both of my parents are black.

If I had a more common name—if I were Denise, Jeanette, or Michelle, as three of my sisters are, I wonder if being asked what I am would bother me. But through some alchemy I don't altogether understand, my name became my shield protecting me from slights or attacks on my essence within. When I turned twelve, I had my hair chemically straightened for the first time. I was so relieved to be free of the nappy mass that I couldn't stop staring in the bathroom mirror and running my hands through the newly silky locks. Then my mother came in. She stood watching me for a few moments before she finally said, deadpan:

"You know you're still just a little nigger girl."

My eyes moved to her reflection in the mirror as she turned and walked away.

I don't know why my mother said what she did. I could speculate that it was her generation's idea that you were supposed to keep children from getting uppity. She could have said it out of jealousy. She could have been expressing some meanness of spirit invoked by a bad memory from her childhood. I don't know and, really, it doesn't matter. I remember this moment not because it was my mother or because of her use of that ugliest of words. I remember it because of what didn't happen: I didn't succumb to the vulnerability of my young age. I didn't accept the "n"-word and the self-loathing that goes along with it. I didn't get angry.

I remember, with some wonder, the response I spoke in my mind, no less matter of fact than my mother's statement. I thought, "No I'm not. I am Sophfronia."

I'm sure that's when I understood, perhaps unconsciously, that it would be vitally important for me to be Sophfronia, and essential to learn what being me means. I am concerned with whether I am being of sound mind, and whether I'm making any progress on the journey that will help me understand God and my relationship with Him. Do I carry myself in such a way that others can know who I am by my spirit and not my color? Martin Luther King Jr. dreamed this for his children, and in my life, it seems, I've molded the content of my character into the shape of my name to the point where I don't identify as a black woman. It's not that I deny I'm a black woman or try to ignore the fact. But it is not the foundation of my identity.

There is a virtue of a name so unique that you can embody it, become it. It's like I had a headstart in defining myself before anyone else could do it for me. This early foundation, I think, contributed to my positive outlook—my name gives me confidence and that confidence makes it easier for me to believe the world is for and not against me. I have built on this foundation, refining the question of who I want to be for myself and others to the point where I have developed this mission: to become so much my name, to fill it with pure soul, that it becomes adjective and more. *I am Sophfronia—That is very Sophfronia—How Sophfronia.* And people who know me know, without question, what that adjective means. They know what it looks like in colors of fire and autumn—they know what it sounds like in a voice as soothing as a memory and a laugh that bubbles downstream like the friendliest of rivers. It is a sense they can't quite put their finger on, but they feel it has always been there, at once familiar and warm. Once a friend wrote a poem for me that said I was a gift . . .

> *giving this same receiver a sense of the divine*
> *in human form*
> *smiling back at him or her.*

I love this idea. If being strong in myself means I get to somehow share with others the presence of Creator Spirit, there has to be something right about how I'm fostering my sense of *Sophfronia*. I'll keep going.

⟨❦⟩

I long for the time when calling someone by his or her first name weighed heavy with meaning. I'm thinking of the time of Austen, of course, and of the Brontës. I remember the moment in *Jane Eyre* when Rochester pleads for Jane to stop calling him "sir." "Say Edward—give me my name—Edward—I will marry you." What was that like, to hear a loved one call you by your given name for the very first time? What trembling was there in the heart, what thrill? It must have been like living behind a veil, semi-invisible, for years and years. Then someone comes along and, in giving voice to your first name, parts the veil and says, "I see you." In this glory you are affirmed and reborn.

I am listening.

> *Do not fear, for I have redeemed you; I have called you by name, you are mine. When you pass through the waters, I will be with you; and through the rivers, they shall not overwhelm you; when you walk through fire you shall not be burned, and the flame shall not consume you . . . you are precious in my sight, and honored, and I love you.*
>
> —Isaiah 43: 1–7

One Sunday after church (my family and I are now members of an Episcopalian congregation) my son and I drove to the hospital to visit a parishioner who had broken her hip in a fall the previous evening. I remember I had all these details rattling around in my brain because it was Easter Sunday and I was tired from attending the Easter Vigil service the previous evening and getting up early for the festival service that morning. We were having guests over for Easter dinner, and my husband had gone home ahead of us to check on the roast in the slow cooker and get the side dishes started. As we walked through the parking garage holding hands, Tain, who was then seven, looked up at me and said, "Mama, do you ever stop to think about how you are the only Sophfronia Scott in this world with your brown eyes and that hair and your being really nice and everything? Did you ever think about how amazing that is, that you're the only one?"

I stopped right then.

Tain appeared the way he always looks with his thoughtful brown eyes full of light and innocent curiosity and his asking such questions all the time. But this was different. I was shocked that I was suddenly not "Mama" but a fully realized person, a person with a name. I was even more shocked that Tain, who never calls me anything but "Mama," chose to call me by my maiden name, which I only use professionally. Hearing my full name sounded by my son's voice rang like a bell in my ear clearing all the distractions from my head and replacing them with something else. *Pay attention. Be here.*

"You know, Tain, I do, but I forget sometimes," I said when I could answer him at last. "That's why I have you and Papa and lots of people who love me to help me remember." And this is true. Hearing my name is how I find my way back to myself.

The first substitute teacher I ever experienced, in first grade, called me "Sophie." I glowered at her, my chin down and arms crossed, for the rest of the day. I haven't allowed anyone to call me Sophie since. This does not mean I shun nicknames—in fact they are true terms of endearment to me. My father called me "Fronia" many times, and my mother and siblings still refer to me as "Fro-Fro" or "Fro." When I played high school basketball in Ohio where I grew up, the nickname "Fronie" came into being and still exists in a certain circle of my friends in New York City where I spent most of my post-college life. Last year I became fast friends with a fellow writer who, both in correspondence and in person, refers to me as "S," and the simplicity of it makes me laugh every time I hear him say "Ess" because I can't believe no one has ever called me by initial before.

Those closest to me, however, even the ones who use nicknames, like my "S" friend, know what it truly means to call me
Sophfronia. I often go long periods of time without hearing my
name, especially in social situations where I'm surrounded by
acquaintances who have forgotten or can't pronounce it and are
too embarrassed to ask me again. When I hear it I light up like a
child whose long lost toy has been returned. No one can comprehend the many acts of love I receive every day simply because I've
heard my name.

A year ago I began to notice how I crave the early morning darkness—not for writing, which has been my habit, but for an odd
kind of walking experience. I get up, usually on a weekend, and
I go downstairs and start to make tea. Then I become aware of a
gorgeous silence filling the air. I'm drawn outside; I feel like I can
step into this silence, this softness. I walk out onto the deck and
stand there, listening. Then I go down the steps, into the driveway.
One morning I found myself outside and down the road before I
realized I was still in my pajamas. It didn't matter. There would be
no one to see me in my oversized New York Jets Training Camp
T-shirt and ratty sweatpants.

On such mornings I am often thinking of Thomas Merton's
Conjectures of a Guilty Bystander, specifically the part called
"The Night Spirit and the Dawn Air":

> The first chirps of the waking birds mark the '*point vierge*' of the
> dawn under a sky as yet without real light, a moment of awe and
> inexpressible innocence, when the Father in perfect silence opens
> their eyes. They begin to speak to Him, not with fluent song, but
> with an awakening question that is their dawn state, their state
> at the '*point vierge*.' Their condition asks if it is time for them
> to 'be.' He answers 'yes.' Then, they one by one wake up, and
> become birds. They manifest themselves as birds beginning to
> sing. Presently they will be fully themselves, and will even fly.

Perhaps the pull I feel on these mornings is my "dawn state."
And maybe I'm sensing the Creator Spirit, walking about giving

the waking birds this vital message, their cue: it is time for them to be. I too want for Him to tell me it is time for me to be.

I go out walking and I am listening. I want to ask a question, like Merton's birds. I don't know what to ask and yet I feel this answer: *I love you I love you I love you.* It is not even a whisper. They are simply words enveloped in the silence and they are out there and in me at the same time. In some ways I am a little girl, walking with my arms out expecting my Daddy to sweep me up into his arms. But in other ways I have blossomed again and again, to the point of pain, in full knowledge of this love. I think I cannot grow or open further. Then I do.

Connecticut's Housatonic River flows less than five miles away. In the early morning it sends fog rolling off its banks to settle on the road below my house. As I head down the hill, the mist shrouds me in oblivion. Every surface of my skin tingles and I know I am waiting—I am waiting to hear my name.

WHITE SHIRTS

When my friend Jenny answered her cell phone that day she said, "I'm walking with Jake and Ella and Grandma in Central Park. We're only a few blocks away, come join us." Jake was Jenny's preschool age son, Ella was her dog, and Grandma? Well, Grandma was Lena Horne—singer, actress, icon. I said okay, hung up the phone, and kept walking but I was pretty sure I'd left part of my brain back on the corner of East 68th and Fifth Avenue. At that point Jenny and I had been friends, dear friends, for close to two years but I'd never met the legendary Lena. Her public appearances, even at family functions, were few. Our mutual friends spoke of her with hushed awe, wondering if they would ever get the opportunity being presented to me then. They talked about the possibilities of being tongue-tied, not knowing what to say, of coming off as being less than fully charged in the mental department. As I walked toward the park I took on all their anxieties, just assuming they were my own. I felt like the suede jacket I broke out each fall suddenly looked shabby, and the scuffmarks on my boots were rising up all white and too obvious.

I found them, stroller, dog, and women, taking up most of a footpath near the East 70s. Jenny introduced me and when Lena said my name "Fronie-Fronie," as I'm known in their family, the fear inside me melted. I recognized the lilt of her voice, but not from her recordings or her movies. She sounded like someone I loved. I heard the tones of my father's sisters during my child-hood: slow and elegant and beautiful.

I don't remember what she wore—unusual for me because at the time I was mad for fashion—but I remember the glow of her skin, the way her chin tilted up to examine my face. Maybe she marveled over my freckles or the reddish brown shade of my dreadlocks. From the intensity of her gaze, though, I gathered that she was searching not for prettiness but for content. She wanted, I think, to see what was in my brown eyes. I remember bearing her weight as she took my arm and we walked while Jenny pushed Jake in the stroller and supervised the leashed but ever-roaming Ella.

I like to believe she spoke to me as she did then because she had soon realized I was not like her granddaughter's other friends, urban and modern and lovely but, for her, out of reach in terms of connections and references. Lena was born in 1917. My father, by then deceased, had come into the world in 1919, so I had grown up with her language, with her references. Talking to her was not that different from talking to my own father in our living room as he sat in his recliner. In fact Lena asked me about "my people" and I told her about my father coming from Mis-sissippi and my mother's family from Tennessee, and how they merged in Ohio but raised me and my siblings as though no one had ever left either of those southern spaces, right down to my father's whippings and demeaning words, which stung even more than the physical strikes. My sisters and I were taught to cook and clean and iron as if they were the only endeavors that could ensure our survival as women. By the time I was 18 and leaving for college I was so angry I vowed never to return. I didn't tell Lena that part.

That's how the ironing talk started. She seemed intrigued that I had learned so young and surprised that I still did it. My husband was, and is, terrible with an iron and it never occurred to me to send the shirts out to be laundered and pressed as most men in New York City, even those who couldn't afford it, probably did. Lena, I learned, had married young, just 19, and to a man who, much like my father, insisted on his wife producing ironed shirts, fresh biscuits, and perfect needlework, but she had been taught none of it. It had been important to her to try, I could see that as a little frown creased Lena's brow. Her own father had been absent most of her childhood and she seemed to have wanted the chance to show this kind of diligence for a man she loved. For a moment Lena released my arm and her pale hands, at waist level, swept through the air in front of her. "I used to weep over that man's shirts," she said. I nodded and we stood there together at an imaginary ironing board. The yellow leaves over our heads and under our feet provided the light for our work on that overcast day. "And they were all white shirts, right?" I asked. I remembered my father's own white shirts as I heard Lena answer, "Yes." We stood there, the shirt large and voluminous in Lena's small hands, the white cotton hopelessly scorched.

Lena had squeezed my heart and I wanted to cry because I could feel how much she had loved her husband, how much she must have tried. I knew what it was to have such obvious proof of failure. I too had burned my father's shirt (and coffee and biscuits and collard greens). But I had been able to make adjustments—so many adjustments—until I had eventually mastered most domestic tasks and could present my father with perfect shirts and perfect biscuits. It never occurred to me what it would have been like never to be able to do it, to never be able to show love in this way. Of course I wouldn't have said that when I was ironing my father's shirts. But I remembered the complete sense of pleasure and satisfaction when my father pulled on a shirt without making a critical remark. Maybe I even felt proud of the way he had looked. I wanted to tell Lena right then how to iron that shirt. Years later it still seemed to matter, and I felt Lena would have listened, that she still wanted to know like it was the answer to an essential, but long-elusive riddle.

To this day I have never read any proper instruction for how to iron a shirt. I suppose if I Googled "how to iron a shirt" I would find enough information, with video included, to bring me to the level of the ironing elite. But I feel what I learned from my mother's hands is old magic—I don't want to meddle with it.

I can tell you I start with the collar, unbuttoning it if it's that kind, and laying it as flat as I can on the ironing board. I press it end to end. Ironing the small parts of a shirt is when you're most likely to get burned. You have to hold the part close to the iron while you press and your fingers are simply in harm's way. A burn rises quickly, a living red capsule on the surface of your skin. You think it will never heal, that's how much it hurts when it happens. Ice is better than butter, I'll tell you that now. Butter and burns is an old wives' tale.

Working with steam is a blessing. I didn't have a steam iron when I was a kid and my arms often ached with the effort of exerting the right pressure to smooth out the fabric. (When I got older my father bought us a Press-O-Matic, a smaller version of the huge rectangular ironing machines you see at the dry cleaners, but that's another story and a different set of burns.) Next I pick up the shirt and lay it on one side of the front with the buttons face down and running horizontally in front of me. I iron that, then the sleeve on that same side. Sleeves are tricky because of their roundness. They don't lie flat well, so I will usually iron a sleeve and turn it over to find a funky crease I didn't mean to create running like a new slash down the arm. Once I fix that I move to the other side and the other sleeve. Then I lay the back of the shirt out with the neck area fitted as much as possible over the narrow end of the ironing board. I press the back and all the little nooks of the back of the neck. I run the nose of the iron around inside the cuffs and then I'm done.

It takes a lot of love to iron a shirt you will never wear. When I see a man wearing a meticulous shirt I wonder who loves him, who has taken the trouble. Or did he have to send the shirt out because no one does?

Thinking about my father now, I tend to focus more on the love and less on the anger. In many ways I have forgiven him. Such forgiveness is possible, I believe, not because he is long dead, but because of these unexpected moments of grace reaching across generations reminding me of this: the reason I hurt so much then was because I cared so much then. I still care. As I look back on that autumn afternoon and how Lena took my arm again as we continued our stroll through Central Park, I can see how in that moment I was in my thirties, Lena was in her eighties, but we were both girls ironing the shirts of the first men we ever cared for, hoping they could feel our love pressed hard into every crease.

PART THREE

THERE ARE ONLY DAYS

TAIN IN THE RAIN

ain didn't come in. The moment the first light raindrops fell, the guests at Patricia Barkman's outdoor art show, many well trained from her past gatherings, had already swept the paintings from their mounts in the garden and rushed them into her studio. More friends picked up dishes, plucked the cloths off the tables, and scurried to get indoors. Then the wind changed in the way that it does when the biggest part of the storm is about to hit, like someone in the sky had turned a big dial all the way up to eleven. It was the kind of wind that makes the trees turn silver because their leaves are being blown so hard you can only see the lighter undersides. Dark gray clouds moved like a thick woolen blanket being pulled over our heads.

I opened the front door of Patricia's clapboard-sided house and looked out over her vast front lawn in search of my seven-year-old son. The lawn ends on the banks of Taunton Lake, where my friend has built a square, wooden pier. There she keeps two Adirondack chairs so she and her husband Leon can sit over the water. I saw Tain standing there, alone on the pier. I stepped outside and my mouth was open and I was just about to call his name to tell him to come in. But I stopped. In that moment I felt this tiny knot of struggle inside me. One part of me, the Mama instinct, wanted to tell Tain to come in. *A storm is coming, it's not safe!* But there was another, quieter, firm voice inside of me, and it was whispering: *Look at your son.*

Tain had his arms held out and he was moving them up and down like he was a human weather vane. At times he put them down and looked out over the lake like he was waiting for a bus to come rumbling down the current. I couldn't translate the language he seemed to be expressing, but I knew this—he was communicating with the coming storm. I felt an excited heartbeat, the kind I don't think I've felt since I was a child. I once marveled at the midday darkness of a threatening cloudburst, just like that. I once knew the enchantment of a wind that seemed to be speaking only to me. I saw that in him. Tain continued to move this way and sway his body like a dancer. My son was feeling the onslaught of the storm.

My hand kept its grasp on the door handle, but I stepped back in and watched through the screen. I couldn't call him in. I knew somehow this was a precious moment. These next few minutes could shape or begin to shape his entire inner life, his connection to the earth, perhaps even his communication with the divine itself. I had to let him do this; I had to let this event unfold.

Wasn't this why we had moved here from New York City in the first place? When Tain was just an infant, no more than two or three months old, my husband and I had taken him for a walk in his stroller in Central Park. As we walked the paths and admired the trees on the verge of autumn splendor, I thought of the little plot of woods behind my parents' home in Lorain, Ohio. I remembered playing out in those woods, alone, in rare moments of privacy away from my six siblings, but within safe earshot of my mother's voice. Out there I made up stories, poked sticks into the ground to pretend I was planting trees, and searched for wild strawberries. In reality I was furnishing my "inside room," that inner sanctum of my mind as described by the young girl Mick Kelly in Carson McCullers's *The Heart Is a Lonely Hunter.* I truly believe the essence of every creative thought that has made me a writer was born out there under the canopy of those unkempt woods.

When we returned from the park to our Upper West Side apartment, I shared these thoughts with my husband. That's when he surprised me: on our walk he had been remembering playing in the fields near his home in Brook Park, Ohio, and wondering, as I did, how we could give Tain this vitally important experience. It just couldn't happen in the city. We looked at each other and in that moment we knew: it was time to go. By January we would call ourselves Newtowners.

That summer day, waiting at Patricia's door, I listened carefully for thunder, but there wasn't any. No sign of lightning either. A cloudburst would definitely drench Tain soon, but I would only stand guard. As long as there was no lightning I would let him be. I figured he would come in when he was ready.

As I stood there, silent guardian that I was, I realized this was the moment I had foreseen in the hospital, just hours after Tain's birth. I remember him glowing in my arms like a newborn star and being shocked by how I didn't feel an ounce of possession about him. All my life I had been hearing people refer to *my son, my daughter,* or *my child* in pride and love, but also with heavy overtones of possession—this is someone who cannot be taken away from me.

But I couldn't bring those words to my mind for Tain. Not in that way. Not ever. This little person in my arms held his own powerful spirit, so big that it was crazy to think I was truly author to this creation. He was himself. Who am I? I am—and I thought this with great humility and gratitude—I am the person blessed with the task of watching over him until he can make his own way in the world. My job would be to guide him, to walk him through all the places he needed to go in order for him to become the person he would become. I have some control and authority, but in the biggest sense I really have none at all. I prayed for help so I would know and accept this and decide accordingly, in Tain's best interest, whenever the important times arose.

And now here, my son perched on the edge of the storm, was one of those moments. Perhaps it was the first of what I knew would be many more in the years to come.

The clouds opened then and the smell of ozone and a wash of water fell across the air. Tain turned and ran toward the house. As he came through the rain I could see on his face this mixture of pride and satisfaction like that of a wizard who had successfully conjured a spell, but also more like a boy who had done something he thought he couldn't do. The look was so strong, so intimate, that I backed away from the door and turned my head so he wouldn't see I had been watching.

LETTER TO A NEWBORN MOTHER

---

*D*ear Maureen,

Yours is absolutely the best news—congratulations! I loved receiving your note, loved feeling the shiny hope of expectation in your words. The knowledge of your past losses and disappointments made it all the more poignant, miraculous even. From now on you have my prayers, thoughts and support every single day as he continues to grow inside you and until you hold him smiling in your arms.

And yes, I suppose now that you are ten weeks away from giving birth, now is the time for us to settle into this old parlor game of asking other mothers for advice. I will indulge you, but I hope I don't disappoint when I say that in my nine years of being a mother and the countless times I've been asked for such advice, my response is always the same:

No one will ever know your child as well as you do.

Yes, read all the books (Sears was a favorite; I never really warmed to Spock), and consult your pediatrician, but at the end of the day, you will know what makes sense for your child because you are the one who sees him most. No one will be closer to your baby. No one will have logged the many hours of close observation that add up to expertise.

I say this because I'm constantly stunned by how many mothers are so willing to let another person's knowledge take precedence over their own where their children are concerned. I would sit at playgrounds and listen to them consult each other endlessly:

"Are you getting the flu shot this year?"

"What are you doing about vitamins?"

"I can't decide if she should be in the morning or afternoon preschool class. Which do you think is better?"

"But Dr. Oz says . . ."

"But Dr. Spock says . . ."

"Well there's an article in *Parenting* that says . . ."

I know it could all be mere small talk. Mothers are always looking for ideas. I've done that. Indeed it was my observation of other babies his age that made me try Tain on solid foods earlier than I had thought possible, and realize he could indeed hang out happily in one of those exer-saucer contraptions while I wrote. But for the most part it really seems to me the mothers I overheard sought permission or validation.

Somehow their behavior is familiar to me and perhaps this is what I'm sensing: they behave as students who haven't prepared for a test. They are students who, up until now, have sat passively in the back of the room of their lives not taking notes. They have known for years that this baby thing might come up, but they have not given thought to who they want to be as mothers or what they need to know to feel confident in the role they envision. But then it's easy to be fooled into thinking someone else has it all figured out and we only need consult the oracles of books, magazines, and YouTube videos. The media has done a thorough job of plastering images of the perfect, contented, Gap-clad baby in our minds like the end result of a completed recipe. Surely if you follow all the bullet-pointed do or don't lists your child will be as happy as the one on the magazine cover. This is the student equivalent of winging it.

But here's the thing—you don't need to immerse yourself in all that media clutter because your child is test, Cliff Notes, and cheat sheet all in one, and rolled up into a cute little ball of help-lessness to boot. He contains all the answers. Study him.

Look at your child. Trust the truth of your own eyes. When my son is not well his skin takes on a pale waxy look. His appetite disappears. He is tired. I'll put him to bed early knowing my husband and I will wake in the middle of the night to a vomiting boy. When Tain is healthy he sports the proverbial rosy cheeks and he eats like he's filling a void for the ages.

When your child is ill you'll find it tempting to give in to the emotion of the situation, but this is exactly when you will need to be fully present and call upon your formidable knowledge of your child. Throughout his early childhood Tain endured a series of ear infections due to having oversized adenoids that kept his ears from draining properly, a trait he inherited from Darryl. We agreed with his pediatrician and ear-nose-throat specialist that we would wait to see if Tain would outgrow the problem before proceeding with a surgical alternative. When he turned six, after a terrible six-week period of ongoing infections and antibiotics we decided it was time for him to have his tonsils and adenoids removed and temporary ear tubes put in place to help with the drainage. That February Tain went into the procedure quite brave, my good little guy, holding on to the stuffed Jesus doll he borrowed from the children's minister at our Episcopal church to keep him company.

Afterward he suffered the usual post-operative pain and discomfort. He seemed bewildered by how much his throat hurt and he cried in that frustrated way a child cries when he has been woken before he was done with being asleep. I knew he was in pain, but there was something else that troubled me—I sensed a sadness about him, almost like a depression. It was as though he had been sucked down into a sinkhole and, if allowed, he would stay down there, crying and contemplating the darkness. While Darryl sat with him and tried to comfort him I went outside and called our friends, the Trottas. Their only child, Thea, is Tain's best friend. They've been joined at the hip since preschool even though they haven't shared a classroom (at the time they attended different private schools and Tain is now in public school) since. I told them Tain was out of surgery, that we would bring him home in a few hours, and asked if it was possible for Thea to come see him. She came and though he couldn't talk to her much, she fussed over him in a way that I'm sure was more fun and more acceptable to him than if I were doing it.

This all happened on a Thursday. The doctor said to expect Tain to be out of school for a week, then he should return for a post-op examination that Friday. But the day after Tain's surgery I, again acting on my instinct, contacted Ms. Coppola, Tain's teacher. My son is an only child, but he is a social child. Something told me his recovery would be better if he could have the company of his friends and enjoy their activity and laughter. At home he would most likely stay on the couch, watch television, and grow sullen. So I told Ms. Coppola I wanted to try to send Tain to school that Monday. I explained what he could and couldn't eat. I spoke to the school nurse as well and informed her of what we were doing and what Tain could have for pain medication if he needed any. Granted, if he were going to the school he attends now, a large bustling public school, I would not have considered this. But at this time he was in a private school, just 8–10 children in his first grade class, and plenty of watchful adult eyes around. From the moment Tain returned his classmates hugged and applauded him as though he were an astronaut back from the moon. They knew of his surgery, an adventure none of them had ever experienced, so they were happy to have one of their own back to tell the tale. The children cared for him too—if they were having snack and one of them noticed only one yogurt left, he or she would grab it for Tain— they all knew he needed to eat soft food. Tain quickly absorbed all the affection of his classmates and picked up the rhythm of school again. For my part I made sure he got plenty of sleep each night and dressed warmly enough in the mornings so he could play outside for recess.

At the end of the week I took Tain to his follow-up appointment, as scheduled, and the doctor marveled at how well he looked. His ears and throat were healing well and Tain was cheerful and glowing.

"He's doing really well," the doctor said. "I don't think I've ever seen a child recover this fast from surgery. What did you do?"

I smiled. "I sent him to school."

Again, dearest, let me point out I'm not telling you to send your child to school immediately post surgery, or that you have to send him to private school. I'm saying pay attention in the moment and sense what he needs. It's not that different from sensing your own. If you are cold, your child is probably cold. If your eyes itch from the air laden with pollen, why wouldn't his eyes feel the same way? Trust your flesh memory. My son is his own spirit, his own person, but he was also once inside my physical being and my flesh remembers him. I pick his nose with no more thought than I would have in picking my own. I hope that doesn't gross you out—I'm trying to make you understand. Actually if you are grossed out I feel sorry for you because you'll have to do much worse than picking noses in the months and years to come! But it really is that simple—you will care for his body the same way you care for your own.

Then again, I could be taking for granted that you and all these mothers I've observed have no issues with sensing your own needs. Perhaps, after all, there is a study or a class one of these mothers skipped out on—the study of herself. She finds it difficult to sense her child's deepest needs because she doesn't know how to pay attention to her own. I guess this shouldn't surprise me. As a society so many of us are disconnected from our bodies both in terms of pain and pleasure. This yawning abyss makes us overeat because we don't sense when we are full, ignore aches that worsen because we leave them untended, and seek medication because we know of no other way to help our bodies feel good and comforted. We don't even realize there could be another way of being.

If you've never studied yourself before, Maureen, you are definitely in the crash course now. What is pregnancy if not an ongoing awareness of how your body is changing day by day? How long after conception did it take you to notice the flat metallic taste in your mouth? And are you craving sugar or salt? So many stories like to perpetuate the image of pregnant women eating bizarre combinations of food—remember the scene in the movie *Junior* where the pregnant Arnold Schwarzeneggar shares a meal with another expectant mom and they devour barbecue wings and a spread of Chinese food in addition to the Italian dinner he cooked earlier? (If you haven't seen the film, I highly recommend it—it's a funny, joyous celebration of life and love, plus watching the Terminator weep from the hormones in his system is simply priceless.) But you'll find your cravings are so much simpler—I needed salt and meat. I pulled out my cast iron Dutch oven and made beef stew every other week. I found deep, satisfying contentment in cheeseburgers with bacon. I never really experienced morning sickness and I wonder now if it was because I gave my body what it needed: salt and iron.

I will admit, I went through some changes that didn't make sense to me—my intolerance for ginger, for one. I loved cooking with ginger, everything from stir-fried vegetables to gingerbread cookies at Christmas. Ginger was also my favorite candle and body butter scent from the Origins store. When I was pregnant, though, the scent of ginger as it traveled through my nasal passages disintegrated into something rancid and irritating. I didn't understand it—ginger usually soothes upset stomachs—but my body rejected it in any form. This sensitivity was slow to go away once I'd given birth.

Observe how your body takes on liquid like a sponge in the two to three weeks before you give birth. No matter how much you want to be or have been the cute pregnant woman looking like a beanpole who's swallowed a basketball, that charade will end when your body begins its final preparations. I weighed in at a solid 180 pounds right after Tain was born. Remember, it is only temporary. If you are aware, and if you'll allow it, your body will let the weight and water go when it realizes it no longer needs the extra padding.

While you are still pregnant you can use the time to decide how you will respond to the comments strangers and loved ones might make. You may already be experiencing this—I lived in New York City during my pregnancy and I found it breathtaking the number of strangers who saw fit to touch my belly and offer their two cents. I'm always stunned by how mindless such comments can be sometimes to the point where I'm sure the person doesn't understand their own utterings. One of my cousins actually confirmed this for me. My son was nearly five months old when we went to visit family in Ohio for Christmas. At one gathering he was crying a lot, most likely because of the noise and the number of people in the room. I decided I would just hold him and keep him close until he settled down.

"Oh, you're going to spoil that baby," my cousin Violet said.

"Spoil him how?" I challenged her. "I didn't have this baby so he could lie in a crib and cry. If he needs to be held, I will hold him."

Violet shrugged uneasily and commented on how that was just what our elders used to say.

I will admit I jumped on her hard. The word "spoiled," used just as she used it, still triggers my annoyance. I heard it a lot in our family when I was little and even then I never liked it. My aunts and uncles especially used the word carelessly, indiscriminately, like an old wives' tale, with no understanding of your relationship with your child or your history of giving or withholding anything.

"I know," I told Violet. "But that doesn't make it right, does it?"

By the way, there will come a time when, if you find it is what your child needs, you will let him lie in a crib and cry so he can learn to fall asleep on his own. But it won't happen until twelve to eighteen months or so, when he realizes it's more interesting to stand up and try to crawl out of the crib than lie down and sleep in it. But your child must learn to sleep properly if you are to maintain your sanity. I say this seriously, dearest. Lack of sleep is the true land mine—people talk about lack of sleep once you have the baby, but really an infant will begin to sleep through the night fairly quickly—Tain started around the three-month mark. It's after, maybe about a year later, when they stop sleeping through the night, when the world drops into a black hole.

Lack of sleep changes you. I mention it here because it will be an obstacle to clear thinking and decision making for your child—and heck, just life in general. I eventually learned never to make any decisions, especially concerning my business, when I was sleep-deprived. I saw everything in a negative light. Prospects I would have entertained before seemed hopeless and not worth the trouble. Everyone, my husband included, seemed thoughtless and unhelpful. That doesn't mean he was, but that was how I felt. I'm sure if this went on for days one might have diagnosed me with depression. But a good night's sleep always changed everything. When Tain started sleeping through the night again Darryl and I felt like new people—shiny, happy people, as the R.E.M. song goes. Whenever I hear of a couple divorcing and learn they have children under the age of three, I wonder if the lack of sleep land mine has tripped them up and blown their personalities out of proportion to the point where they simply don't like each other anymore. I want to tell them to wait, sleep on it, maybe for a week, and see how they feel about their marriage after catching up on their Z's.

When I haven't slept my brain feels like a thorny burr inside my head. I can't bear to connect with it. I don't want to think let alone dream. And yet I must function so I do—but I am prickly because my brain is prickly so it is hard for anyone like my poor husband to connect with me. I am also tired from making a concerted effort not to be prickly with my son. I acted in my share of silly scenes pleading with the baby to go to sleep, that Mama was simply exhausted. One night, at 2 a.m., in an effort to lull him to sleep I took him downstairs to sit with me in the window seat of our family room to stare at the gleaming cookie of a full moon in the dark sky. I know books say I should have kept him in his bed, but it felt right for us to sit and look at the moon and we did so. I can't tell you when he finally went to sleep that night, but I cherish the memory of watching that full moon with him. I like to think I made a good call then.

Maureen, I know what it's like to carry a baby after experiencing miscarriage. I know it's hard to be hopeful, to believe that each cell of the precious being inside you is truly knitting together as it should, sight unseen. But I encourage you with all my heart and soul to believe in your son's life. You have already spent so much time in sad realms where you had no chance to develop and nurture such a belief. You don't have to dwell there anymore. Don't be afraid anymore. There's a lyric from a song in in the musical of the book *Jane Eyre* that goes,

> *I know you're afraid*
> *I'm as scared as you are*
> *But willing to be brave,*
> *Brave enough for love.*

Be brave, Maureen. Brave enough for love. You'll soon learn you must be brave for your child in many, many instances. This is where you begin. I know you can do this. I'm glad you like that wonderful picture of Tain from last year's Christmas card. Yes, keep using Tain as your inspiration. He is most certainly mine.

Please keep me posted.

Much love to you and yours,

Sophfronia

PRECIOUS CARGO

T o be a substitute school bus driver is a heartbreaking proposition. Or maybe it was just that way for me. Two years ago I spent a year transporting kindergarten through high school-aged students to and from their homes in their annual 180-day journey to becoming educated. I would like to think I am an educated adult or, at the very least, I was an educated bus driver. But then it seems every education leaves so many important pieces unlearned. The trainers in the bus driving classes, for example, didn't tell me what might happen to my heart as a result of the osmotic process of spending my mornings and afternoons with so many young people. They only stress being the boss of your bus, and how you have to make sure the students sit down and follow all safety rules. The trainers are concerned with helping you pass the initial written test at the Department of Motor Vehicles so you can obtain your learner's permit and get your road training hours in, especially on the cone- and flag-marked static course where you learn—though it seems improbable at first—how to parallel park a seventy-seven-passenger, forty-foot

long school bus. No one tells you how, when you're a substitute
school bus driver, you must walk in this odd duality where on one
level you care deeply and intensely about the welfare of your precious cargo, but on another level you are not to care at all.

I'd been driving my son to and from his private school, twenty
minutes away by way of I-84, for three years. When his move to
public school for third grade coincided with the district's need for
new bus drivers, my husband and I thought this would be an ideal
part-time job for me. I would drive to and from school, which I
already did, and have the hours in between to write. It seemed
like an ideal situation. My only worry was whether or not I could
really handle such a large vehicle, a concern that disappeared the
moment I first strapped myself in the seat. As it turned out, the
feeling was all too familiar. I had spent my teenage years maneu-
vering the roads of my hometown, Lorain, Ohio, in a fifteen-passenger, extended-rear 1979 Plymouth Voyager. This monster of a
van was once commonly used for transportation at churches and
schools but for my family, with its brood of seven fast-growing
children in the age before minivans and suburb-friendly SUVs, the
Voyager was our family vehicle. My father, who loved accessoriz-
ing, festooned it with American flags on the dual rear antennae,
and a huge set of fog lights on top. The kids at school called it
the Scottmobile. Despite the usual embarrassment that came of
being a teenager wishing I could drive to school in a cute com-
pact Toyota or a Ford Escort, I did enjoy sitting so high above
the road—I could see everything. The 10'6" tall school bus felt
just as comfortable, and I had the same sense that if I was careful
in how I positioned myself in the lanes and aimed the nose of the
bus appropriately for where I wanted to go, the rest of the vehicle
would follow.

Many days during the training and long after I earned my
commercial drivers license, I'd board the bus and hear my father's
voice in my mind with his old reminder:

"You know this is no little ass car you're driving, don't you?"

"Yes, sir."

Maybe having the voice of my first and strictest driving
instructor in my mind helped. I mastered the skill set quickly,

including the verbal aspects of the testing. Many new drivers fal-
ter in the first part of the final examination when they have to
walk the DMV inspector through all of the finer points of the
pre-trip inspection that a driver must perform before taking a bus
out, and do it in less than twenty minutes. I could point out how
the front tires must have 4/32nds of tread (no recaps or retread-
ing allowed on the front tires, but it's okay for the rear ones),
the rims must have no cracks or welds, the tire wall must be in
good condition, and the valve stem straight and capped. I'd show,
among other things, how to kick the steering mechanism on the
left front tire, open the battery compartment to check for leaks
and corrosion, and point out how the exhaust pipe must not
extend more than two inches from the rear bumper of the bus.
Inside I performed a full air brake inspection (example: when I
apply the foot brake, my air tanks cannot lose more than three psi
in one minute), checked all windows for cracks and the seats for
signs of vandalism. I made sure that the emergency exits were all
marked and that buzzers sounded when I opened them—with the
emergency windows I remember to use my weaker, not-dominant
hand when opening them, and I ensure that they swung freely.

I acquired my commercial drivers license in October, and from
then on my family's days began in darkness. I lived by the inexo-
rable ticking of the clock, rising from bed, getting dressed, and
then doing whatever cajoling, prodding, and reminding was necessary to get my son up, fed, and dressed so we could make it to
the bus lot by 5:45 a.m. and see what the morning held in store
for us. My husband, a middle school band director in a different school district, would leave the house just 15 minutes after
we did. At the office I'd receive route sheets for a driver who, for
one reason or another, couldn't drive that morning. Most of the
routes started between 6 and 6:20 a.m., so no matter what the
assignment, I'd have to go out, perform the inspection, and hit the
road pretty quickly with only a few minutes to consult a map if I
didn't know the neighborhood in question. Our buses didn't have
GPS systems and using the navigation on cellphones was out of
the question because, by company policy, our phones had to be
turned off while we drove. I'd pick up and deliver the high school
and middle school students first, then do the intermediate school

(grades 5–6), followed by the elementary school last. The noise level rises like the tide as the morning wears on. The teenagers board sleepy and silent, hooded like monks in their sweatshirts, clutching thermoses of hot coffee. As the sun rises a few of them may open their lips and murmur to each other in ready acknowledgment of the coming day. Just an hour later the intermediate students will pour out chatter of bragging and gossip, and by 8:30 a.m. the elementary children are bustling up the steps and filling the bus, like a balloon of life, full of laughter and singing. I have time for one break in the morning, but if the bus I'm driving is bound for one of the three area elementary schools that is not my son's, I spend the off time walking him across the parking lot of the Fairfield Hills municipal center, where many drivers took their breaks, to find a bus that was headed to his school. At this point he has already spent over two hours on the bus reading or playing games and watching videos on my phone (that was allowed). When he says good-bye I worry about how sleepy he will be after he's had lunch in the afternoon.

Driving routes on unknown roads meant I had to navigate new hazards daily. As much as I knew my reference points on the bus and had practiced a variety of maneuvers, one day I managed to hit a short post while backing up. Another time I scraped a mailbox. These minor mishaps are somewhat expected of new drivers, but there is one thing we must do perfectly, every single time, without question. Morning and afternoon, no matter the route, the essence of bus driving is this: the pick up and the drop off.

When picking up children my right hand stays on the steering wheel while my left hand glides over to the control panel so, when I get to within 100 feet of the bus stop, I can switch on my amber warning lights. I take a quick glance at "ELMO," the external light monitoring system that tells me, with a set of blinking yellow dots, my ambers are indeed on and working. I check my mirrors, rear zone and speed control, pulling to the right as safely as possible. I count the number of children at the stop as I approach, stopping the bus within ten feet of them. I activate my stop sign, crossing bar, and red SOS lights, again checking ELMO, this time for the telltale red dots that told me the lights on the outside are working. I secure the bus by putting on my parking brake and shifting into neutral. I keep one hand on the horn and my foot on the brake. If the children need to cross the street in order to board the bus, I look to ensure that traffic has stopped in all directions. When I know it's clear, I will give a big head nod so they know it's okay to cross. You don't give hand signals. For one, you really can't—you have one hand on the horn and the other hand on the switch operating the door—and second, a hand signal can be misconstrued. A car might think you're waving them on to pass you. If their regular driver has trained them well at the beginning of the school year, the children know to look for the nod. I count the children as they cross the street; I count them again as they board the bus, closing the door when the last child reaches the top step. While they get seated I scan all my mirrors, checking for traffic and late-comers. I end my scan with the rear-view mirror above my head to make sure all the children are sitting. Then I put the bus in drive, release the parking brake, pull in my stop sign, turn on my left turn signal, and move the bus slowly, performing the "five-second crawl" in which my head moves back and forth, scanning the crossover mirrors on the nose of the bus to make sure there are no obstructions in front of me. I end my scan with my left mirror as I pull into the road again and proceed. I make sure I remember to cancel my turn signal.

For all the times I count children, as a substitute driver, for the most part, I do not know their names. This, not to mention the daily stress from the lack of routine, bothered me and made me doubt the work. But one day my friend Jane, a woman so caring and full of common sense that my husband and I refer to her as Bodhisattva Jane, said being a substitute bus driver was like having a mission, and that my cheerful demeanor probably helped in ways I may never realize—that in my determination to smile at all the children who board my bus, I might smile at someone who might not get a smile during the normal course of their day. And this would be good for me as well. Annie Dillard once wrote, "Never, ever get yourself into a situation where you have nothing to do but write and read. You'll go into a depression. You have to be doing something good for the world, something undeniably useful; you need exercise, too, and people." Driving the school bus took me out of my writer head, and ensured I had to engage in the world for six hours every day.

In certain aspects I drove my bus as if I were driving my son alone. I would call out, "Oh, look, a fox!" to forty kids the same as I would to my son. Happily, small faces would respond, and turn to the windows just as he would. I pointed out rainbows over Taunton Lake, a deer and her fawn by the side of the road, and the tiny airplane whose owner takes off from a field on Orchard Hill Road. I liked how the children responded in fascination despite the fact that these were their home roads, and they traveled the route more than I did. I liked how if I were open to wonder, they could be too.

Still, the absence of names troubled me. It's hard to ask a kid in the back of the bus to sit down if you don't know their name. There was an inconsistency across the board with how some drivers ran their buses, so I was often put in the position of being the "mean" substitute not allowing students to do things that were perfectly fine before, like having their feet in the aisles, or being on their knees to talk to the friend in the seat behind them. I grew painfully aware of the challenge of daily seeing new children without ever getting to know them as a teacher would. I know this would be different if I had a regular route. One longtime driver told me how much he enjoyed "working with the children," and I took this to mean helping them to develop some awareness, perhaps an awareness they can carry into their everyday lives. Because most of the unsafe behavior children do on a bus—and off a bus (as a parent I know this for a fact)—happens from simple inattention. The kid in the seat behind is playing a handheld video game, a sound goes off that indicates he's reached a new level, the boy in the seat in front of him recognizes the sound and wants to see how he did it. Suddenly he's up and kneeling on his seat so he can look into the seat behind him, even if the driver has asked him to sit down only five minutes earlier. It's not disobedience—just thoughtlessness. It takes daily patience, patience I knew the longtime driver to have, to deliver the repeated reminders, to not grow frustrated or lose one's temper. It's like the daily tending of a flower with only the slightest hope that your watering, fertilizing, and careful pruning will yield a beautiful blossom.

And yet I seemed to want the opportunity to have my own route and to do this tending. It's the mom in me that wants to see the kids enough to praise them when they behave well on the bus, to ask a child about the project she's carrying, to say "welcome back" after a school vacation.

Though I was a substitute I drove almost every day, even if I was just shuttling buses forty-five minutes up to the maintenance garage for repair. Sometimes I was gone all day with an out-of-town field trip, or taking a team to a meet after school. But everything tapered off just before the holidays. The drivers were all determinedly present then. They wanted to make sure they were there to collect the many gifts students and parents had waiting for them. As a substitute driver I get no gifts and no acknowledgement even though I, like the regular drivers, have driven all of these children, to school, to nature preserves, to hockey games, to tennis meets and color guard competitions. It's not that I care so much about receiving the cards or the cookies or the fruitcake. But I do miss the relationships these gifts represent. The futility of the job seemed to me most pressing, and I was on the verge of quitting. But then, at Christmas Eve service at my church, a little girl who sings in the choir with my son and whose route I had driven a few times presented me with a miniature metal school bus ornament tied with a blue ribbon. I accepted it with tears in my eyes and considered it a sign I should continue. I carried it in my bus bag for the rest of the school year.

And because I stayed I eventually had the pleasure of new and special experiences. Once I happened to drive a route for a driver who was out sick for a week. On the afternoon high school run, a student—he said his name was Matt—boarded the bus and said to me, "With our regular driver I usually sit behind her and play music for her." Our buses have no regular radios, only the kind that allows us to communicate to the office.

"That would be fine with me," I said. "I like music too."

Matt fired up his mp3 player and held it just behind my seat to the left. I discovered he liked to talk about music as well. He told me where the Linkin Park album we were listening to fell in the chronology of the band's discography. He explained the merits of certain songs he liked, at times in anticipation of a song so

I would know what to listen for when it began. I heard him in grateful wonder—this same student barely spoke a word in the mornings, perhaps he was barely awake—but after school Matt proved to be thoughtful and attentive. He would tell me which students were absent so I wouldn't have to make unnecessary stops. He would ask if there was any music I preferred because he would gladly download it. I told him I'd rather hear what interested him, and this was true. For all I knew, this could be the only time he had the opportunity to voice his passion. I read *Jane Eyre* at thirteen and had to wait three years before I met another student my age who could discuss it with me. One day, long after his driver had returned, I saw Matt in a parking lot and called out to him to say hello. He was surprised I remembered his name. I was thinking how happy it made me to have his name to remember.

One afternoon I arrived at a child's home, opened the bus door, and told him I was so glad to see him again, and I hoped he enjoyed the rest of his day. But he didn't bounce down the steps and onto his driveway like I've seen other children do. He stood next to me and seemed sad, his downcast eyes calling attention to the blondeness of his lashes.

"Will you be our bus driver from now on?" he asked.

I had driven his route two days in a row, but already he was the third child to make this inquiry and I had noticed how the parents seemed so happy when I waved to them—they responded more energetically than I was accustomed to, so I finally said, "Why, honey? Do you need a new driver?"

He nodded. "Yes," he replied. "Our other driver doesn't talk to us."

My heart ached for all of them—driver, parents, and children. I wanted to intervene, to be the bridging empathy that might allow them to reach each other. I knew their driver, and the person was in truth quite nice. Apparently something had happened to form the rift, but whatever it was did not and could not include me. It was like watching a leak in a levee when you might be able to patch it, but you're not allowed because it's not your job to do so.

When I substitute for beloved drivers, though, I cannot do well enough. My arrival times are either too early or too late for the parents and students, and I must hear every day questions of where the other driver is and when she will return. But I'm never privy to such information. I can only tell them, "She will be back. I just don't know when."

What is my job? I think about vocation—I could easily make this my vocation for the next thirty years, drive a school bus while spending the rest of my time writing. But I have a new understanding of vocation since reading Thomas Merton's autobiography, *The Seven Storey Mountain,* and how he sought to understand whether or not the priesthood was his true vocation. For him vocation was not just a matter of a job or even a "calling," which is the word one usually hears about entering the spiritual life. Instead, Merton uses the words "desire" and "hopefulness" when speaking of vocation. It seems to me that vocation isn't a matter of what you can do or even what you're supposed to do—it's about what you are drawn to because it is who you are, so much so that to be in your true vocation is to find wholeness because your vocation is you, right down to the depths of your soul.

I have not pursued any number of activities in recent years because I had already sensed this without knowing why. I've been encouraged to get my teacher certification in yoga and even came close to registering for the class to acquire it. I know my way around bicycles, both real and stationary, so well that I once stepped in and taught a spinning class when the teacher didn't show up. "You could be a trainer," someone said. Yes. I could see myself doing these things and enjoying them. The question in my mind was, "Am I supposed to be doing this?" Perhaps I sensed the absence of the mysterious magnetic pull that I believe indicates vocation. Am I supposed to be driving a bus? The mother in me thought, "Yes." When Jane spoke to me of mission and how bus driving could be mine, I thought, "Yes." But even as I was doing it, I would miss a couple of days a month to teach a workshop, attend a reading, or meet with my literary agent in New York City. These breaks, I have to admit, made it possible for me to keep going. These activities, and not bus driving, reminded me of who I am—a writer. They suspended me above the abyss of negative energy that threatened whenever I became so exhausted I could barely read, let alone write. Many times I felt as though I hadn't really lived those driving hours of my life—I had only "gotten through" another day. When I learned at the beginning of the following school year that such breaks meant I wouldn't, though I had expected it the whole summer, be assigned my own route, I was angry but not devastated. When I had to decide whether to remain a substitute driver and endure the ongoing frustrations and the tired look of my son's afternoon eyes, or leave, it was all too easy to go.

The only thing I regret is no longer transporting such precious cargo. I still think about taking students to New Haven on field trips, driving over the Stevenson Dam in the morning, the red trunks of the evergreens standing sentinel as the narrow roadway passed over the trapped waters of the Housatonic River. The sun streaming over us seemed to bless everything it touched with the glow of possibility. I would drive slowly over the towering, rushing wall of water for safety reasons, of course, but also because I hoped the children were noticing how we were, in that moment, like hawks flying so high over beauty, higher than they could ever fly in their parents' SUV. If a child noticed that, perhaps even enough to remember it and write about it someday, then that would be a truer gift to him or her, with more lasting effects, than any smile of mine could ever deliver.

THE PAYOFF LETTER

Chase Home Finance
3415 Vision Drive
Columbus OH 43219
800–689–9136 Customer Care
800–689–0542 TDD / Text Telephone

April 1, 2012

Sophfronia Scott
62 Turkey Hill Road
Sandy Hook, CT 06482

Re: Home Mortgage Loan # ******2542
Payoff Letter

Dear Sophfronia Scott:
This letter is to acknowledge that Chase Home Finance (Chase)
has received the funds to pay off your mortgage loan referenced
above. Chase will forward an original executed release of lien for

recording to the recorder's office in the county where the property is located.

Until the release is processed, this letter will serve as proof that Chase has received the payoff funds. Within 30 days from receiving the payoff funds, Chase will forward any funds we receive in excess of the payoff amount and any remaining escrow funds for you. Unless notified of an address change, Chase will send the overpayment or escrow refund you are entitled to as a result of this payoff and your 1098 year-end interest statement to the mailing address used for sending this letter. To prevent a delay, please inform us of any change in your mailing address, but since your goal has been to always remain in this home such a change is highly unlikely.

You may contact the county or town recorder's office for information about the time to process the lien release and how to obtain a recorded copy.

If Chase collected escrow funds for paying your mortgage taxes or insurance, you are now responsible for the payment of these items. Please contact your homeowner's insurance agent and your taxing authority to advise them of the address to forward future bills and correspondence. As long as these payments are kept current—they are usually made on a yearly basis—you will not have to fear losing your home as was your concern each month when your mortgage payment came due.

You may now tell your son you have increased the probability that he can remain in the home for his entire childhood, and he will most likely have a tidy inheritance coming his way, depending on the health of the real estate market, when he is grown and you and your spouse are deceased. He may continue to tack up with pushpins, and not wall putty, the posters and drawings he makes for his room. The holes in the drywall do not seem to bother you as it does other parents and, after all, the walls are now yours. When he is a teenager, he may want to paint his room something other than the sunny yellow you thought appropriate when he was a baby. A gentle reminder for him to apply a bit of spackle to the tiny perforations before he does so should be adequate. The color black should be discouraged as rigorously as possible.

You are likely also thinking of the pencil markings in the basement mudroom, indicating the increase in your son's height from the age of two. No one will paint over them now, at least not for many more years, unless you choose to do so yourself.

It is recommended, however, that a thorough de-cluttering take place at least once a year, focusing on the attic and basement spaces. This will prevent the property from developing hoarding issues and keep your home comfortable for years to come. Clutter accumulates in a more determined fashion when a family raises a child from infancy in one house. The four plastic storage bins of clothing, labeled with masking tape "0–3 months" and "6–9 months," for example, are no longer necessary. If you were going to pass them on to a friend or family member, you would have done so by now. Goodwill (www.Goodwill.org) or Big Brothers Big Sisters (www.bbbs.org) will arrange a home pickup for your convenience.

If you cannot bear to discard any of your son's belongings after he has grown up and left the home, we suggest you ship them to his house to dispose of as he chooses.

But perhaps it is wrong to focus on this when all you really care about is the new certainty that you will always have your office, the red room with the yellow chaise and the connected library with the wall of books and your writing table. All this time you feared losing it when all you really had to do was let go of it and write.

This is the space that matters to you most. The large window with the plastic white lines that make it look like separate panes of glass frames the sun rising over the hill in the woods in the morning to shine on your desk just so. It is fitting to have such big windows, especially in autumn when the yellow leaves just outside blaze and fire your creativity. But then all windows are important to you. You moved into this house in January 2005, with a six-month-old infant and only one car. Your one requirement was that the home be light and airy enough that no matter how long you spent in it each day with your baby you would never feel confined. The house turned out to be so bright, in fact, that you can follow the sun all around the property if you like, but these days you can stay in your office. This is the room where you sit on red cushions in a corner to pray like Thomas Merton, and you nap on the chaise like George Sands, and at your desk you write your letters like Anais Nin. It is yours now for as long as you like.

Your spouse, likewise, can keep the odd, sapphire blue color in his basement recording studio although, if forced to sell, you were more concerned with having to take down the extra walls and soundproofing he installed to create his perfect haven. You will still hear the sounds of hesitant trombonists beneath your feet as he teaches private lessons. You will also, unfortunately, have that eerie sense of a voice coming through the walls until you remember it's most likely his muffled singing as he rehearses for his next gig. Please try to keep in mind your home is not haunted nor is there any record of it ever having been so.

Since you know you will stay in this house now you must be more vigilant in regularly cutting back the row of dwarf lilac bushes in front of the house. Otherwise they will become overgrown and you will have to admit neglect and defeat and have the bushes removed. You did not pay off your mortgage to experience such heartbreak.

Chase's goal is to provide the highest level of quality service to each of our customers. If you have any questions, please contact Customer Care at 800–689–9136.

We appreciate the opportunity to have serviced your mortgage loan and hope that you will contact Chase for your future financial needs.

Sincerely,
Reconveyance Department, Chase Home Finance
Reconveyance Services for Alaska, Nevada and California are provided by J. P. Morgan Chase Custody Services, Inc.

TONI MORRISON AND ME

I tend to talk about Toni Morrison with a cautious blitheness. I mention how we share the same hometown, Lorain, Ohio, but even that's a scary thing to do. Why would I want to invite comparisons to a Nobel and Pulitzer Prize–winning author? Such a thought would send most writers under their desks, possibly holding a thick reference book over their heads, like we used to do for tornado drills in my old elementary school, as protection from the debris surely to fly around them. However, when I saw the video of Ms. Morrison's interview with Stephen Colbert, I realized it's time for me to talk seriously about what binds me to this important author and how she taught me something about myself that makes me confident, not fearful, in my work.

When Colbert asked how Ms. Morrison wanted to be "pigeon-holed" if not as an African-American writer, she said she wanted to be known "as an American writer." She went on to say, "There is no such thing as race. None. There's just the human race. Racism is a construct, a social construct. . . ." I agreed and knew what she meant from the fiber of my being. I too think of myself as simply "a writer" working from the imagination and experience of being a human who happens to be named Sophfronia Scott. I have always felt this way, but up until about ten years ago I couldn't "own" it because I didn't understand it. I only knew from a very young age I didn't see the world along racial lines and thought this was an awareness I somehow missed out on. When I was in high school I often heard whispers that I wasn't "black enough" or that I didn't "sound black." This led me to wonder if I was lacking in a way I could never figure out how to fix.

But then I happened upon Hinton Als's 2003 profile of Toni Morrison in *The New Yorker.* I discovered she and I, despite our age difference, have a lot more in common than I knew, and these similarities were most likely what had shaped my worldview. It began with the most basic of shared characteristics—our fathers both worked at U.S. Steel, and she and I both grew up hanging clothes to dry outside, doing it very badly at times, and coming to a realization early on that we would not have the same existence as our mothers and aunts.

"I developed a kind of individualism—apart from the family—that was very much involved in my own daydreaming, my own creativity, and my own reading. But primarily—and this has been true all my life—not really minding what other people said, just not minding."

But the big thing she pointed out to me in this article was how our community in Lorain was so integrated. *Morrison always lived, she said, "below or next to white people," and the schools were integrated—stratification in Lorain was more economic than racial.* The piece also noted the work at U.S. Steel attracted not only American blacks from the South (my father was from Mississippi) but also displaced Europeans: Poles, Greeks, and Italians. The city has a large Hispanic population as well. This made me think of my father's Polish friends we used to visit and of Lorain's annual International Day Festival. To me this was just the way I grew up—I didn't know I was living an integrated existence, or even what it meant.

Then, to match our outer experience, it seems Morrison and I fed our minds a creative diet that turned out to be just as integrated. *As a child, Morrison read virtually everything, from drawing-*

room comedies to Theodore Dreiser, from Jane Austen to Richard Wright. I had done the same, thoroughly steeping myself in the work of Brontë (Charlotte and Emily), Austen, Dickens, Tolstoy, Flaubert, Wright, Ellison, and, yes, Morrison. My influences cover the globe.

I realized I come by honestly my inclination to write from views and voices not my own. The characters in my fiction are white and black, gay and straight, of various religions and nationalities. I used to worry about being taken to task for this and that I wouldn't have the confidence to back up this tendency because I didn't understand it myself. But Morrison helped me to see this inclination is truly my own. I have been nurtured by my inner and outer environments to write this way, and once I knew this I could write with confidence and without apology. And in all this writing I know I am seeking to tell one humanistic story and it is and will always be, I think, a love story. Morrison's stories also seek such basic humanistic elements: love, mercy, forgiveness.

So if you ask me whether I aspire to be like Toni Morrison, I would say this: I don't aspire to her lyricism or style, which are very much her own, but I do have this simple ambition—to tell a good story and tell it well. This aspect, I think, is where she and I both come from, the true hometown we share.

TO WINTER WARMING

J remember reading the story "The Little Match Girl"
when I was about five or six years old and being confused
by the ending. How could the girl be taken up into her
grandmother's firelight embrace and then be found on the cold
street in the morning? Likewise I didn't understand the "Blizzard"
episode of the television show *Little House on the Prairie* when
Laura and her sisters and classmates walked home from school
straight into a snowstorm, and Pa and Mr. Edwards and all the
other fathers covered their heads in hats and scarves and trudged
out into the wind in search of their offspring. One man, who
seemed especially disheartened, lay down alone in the snow and
removed his scarf and opened his coat. I didn't know what he was
doing, only that he didn't come back even after they found the
children and everyone else was safe. Then in school I read Jack
London's "To Build a Fire," and learned the awful truth: winter
can kill. It didn't matter how bundled up you were—low temperatures and long exposure brought the same results: frostbite,
loss of extremities, defeat of the senses, and death. I felt betrayed,

betrayed by visions of sugar plums and Christmas and hot chocolate, betrayed by every cheerful Currier & Ives sleigh bells tin-
kling scene, betrayed by every department store advertisement
that makes it seem like you would be perfectly fine and perfectly
warm in winter weather if you had this parka with the fur-
trimmed hood, and those gloves with the thick fleece lining and
that hat with the convenient flaps to cover your ears. And had my
body always known this was a lie? My middle and ring fingers on
both hands turn yellowish-white from the slightest kiss of frost.

Over the years I have wrestled with this sense of betrayal and
tried to reconcile myself to winter. But the result is a love-hate
mishmash and so I've come to consider winter to be the season
of negative capability. It is beautiful and bare, magically soft and
treacherously dangerous. I have seen in winter the promise of life
from the first shoots of Lenten roses poking through the snow,
but I've also experienced grievous, senseless death. I have some
acceptance of this duality, but I realize my issues with winter go
far beyond whether I love it or hate it, or how cold I am in any
given moment. I've been struggling against a bigger feeling, a concern perhaps, and it is as simple (or complicated, depending on
how you see it) as this: When it's cold, God is not here. That's
what I feel though it doesn't make sense. Of course God is everywhere. But I also equate God with light. On a persistently gray
day, when I look out of my window into the woods behind my
house and see nothing but the black bark of the trees standing
naked in the gloom, I don't see God.

The only exception in this: One night in college I walked
out onto the surface of a frozen river. Arctic-level temperatures
gripped the area for days so the fact of this ice and that others
walked across it every day held no magic in the matter. On that
night, though, as the sky truly was midnight blue, darker than
the Crayola crayon I loved best, and the stars were so white they
spotted the night like bursts of snow, I walked upon that ice and
felt upheld and safe. I stood on the palm of a great hand stretched
out just for me, and I could sense someone's delight, someone's
promise that, "It's okay, I've got you." I almost couldn't breathe,
but what took my breath, exactly? Was it the bitter cold or divine
love and wonder? I know I felt love—I will even say I felt God. As

much as it seems to me God is absent in winter, while I stood on that ice He seemed achingly present. I keep that night in my coat pockets, a kind of hand warmer as I walk through years of cold days equivocating over my feelings about winter.

In the summer and fall the woods behind our house are like a second home. Walking up the slope my son disappears behind a curtain of leaves and plays on the trunks of fallen trees and laughs freely with his friends because they have forgotten I am still so close and can hear them from where I sit on our deck. I walk into this room of largesse in the mornings after putting him on the school bus, and sit on a rock in meditation. This space is like the answer to those dreams most often had by the dwellers of small New York City apartments, that you have a room in your home, extra precious space you didn't know about or somehow missed before. In the winter, the trees stripped, the room is open to the world like a glass house. I don't go in there in the winter because I can't bear to be seen—part of the enticement is the allusion of solitude and Walden-like silence. It's hard to feel that when I can see that blue house even though it is miles away and invisible three quarters of the year. Annie Dillard wrote, "All that summer conceals, winter reveals," and this is true. We are not the only ones uncovered, undone. In the winter my son points to the many birds nests, newly visible, in the trees in our yard, and I get the sense that without realizing it we've been living in a public housing development full of unknown lives.

I believe if I couldn't see the homes of our neighbors as I can see these nests I might feel more comfortable in the bareness. If I had, let's say, the forty-six acres on which, in 1949, the architect Philip Johnson built his famous glass house in New Canaan, Connecticut, I would happily sit exposed because I would be too far away for any prying eyes to see me. The glass house sits perched on a hillside that falls down and away toward a pond and a stand of magnificent trees. Johnson liked to say he had "expensive wallpaper," and I would add to that "exquisite." I have stood in the bedroom area for as long as the tour guide allowed, long enough to sense my belonging, as I watched the sun beginning its drop toward the trees and tinge their barks golden. But then I've only visited the property in summer and early autumn. I don't know what the glass house feels like in winter, when the occupant must look out on endless gray days and the light takes its leave by 5 p.m. I have seen photographs where it seems the heavy snow-laden clouds might crush the glass jewel box; and I've seen pictures where the home reflects the glory of a deep, deep blue January sky. How did Johnson take all this in? Did he write his lover's name in the hoary frost on the glass each morning? Did he light the fireplace in the round brick cylinder, the only opaque wall in the house, and sit staring into the flames with his back to the snow? I think it would make me want to wear a coat in the house all day long, no matter how well heated it was.

The winter of 2010–2011 dumped seven feet of snow on the state of Connecticut over the course of a series of storms that marched across the Northeast, one after the other, leaving residents breathtakingly overwhelmed. As each weather system formed I would watch the day's news reports and laugh about how in the days before Christmas some mothers at my son's school had gathered in the parking lot after dropping off our children and discussed how they yearned for a white Christmas. They received their wish, but it was a day late in coming. On December 26 the storm known as the Boxing Day Blizzard pummeled us and the winter just skidded downhill from there. I grew up in Lorain, Ohio, where lake-effect snow could gather strength over Lake Erie and drop copious amounts of the white stuff in a short amount of time; we were practically ground zero for the great Blizzard of '78, but winter 2010–2011 eclipsed all memories of that legendary snow. During one storm in late January the snow fell in parts of Connecticut at a rate of nearly four inches an hour. Our suburban street seemed like a new city, the road lined with stunning palaces constructed of five-foot-high walls of snow pushed into place by the plows. At one point my husband Darryl and I had to shovel a tunnel-ish path from our driveway, up the back steps and across our deck so the oil deliveryman could pull his hose through the narrow passageway to fill our tank. In other homes oil tanks ran dry because the owners couldn't move the snow themselves and anyone they could have paid to do it was already too busy.

Some plow drivers broke their equipment in the heavy snow and often found themselves stranded as well.

Annie Dillard wrote, "the wind won't stop, but the house will hold," but in January 2011 you couldn't rely on the house part. Ancient barns collapsed all over the countryside from the weight of the snow and homeowners feared the same fate for their dwellings. We learned about roof rakes then, a rectangular piece of metal or plastic like a tiny bulldozer attached to the end of a long angled pole. You reached up with it and pulled the snow toward you and off the roof to keep your house from caving in—still not an easy process, especially if you were already standing hip deep in snow and pulling two feet more on top of you. Throughout my childhood in Ohio, including the Blizzard of 1978 when we shoveled our driveway so many times there was no place to put the snow, we never cleared snow from our roof. What new devilry was this? Hardware stores couldn't keep the roof rakes in stock. We managed to procure one and my husband did clear our roof a few times. We haven't used it since.

Our friend James became the expert on roof rakes and the happy loaner of his own in his neighborhood. "Ace Hardware in the center of town has thirty-six roof rakes now," he said in a matter-of-fact way as he adjusted his wireframe glasses on the bridge of his nose. He was right, as always, and that's when we bought ours while replenishing our supply of ice melt for the driveway. When our families got together we would discuss with James the dangers of climbing a ladder in such snow trying to reach the second story of our houses, but a necessity when ice dams formed along the gutters. We saw light brown clouds of water stains in two bedrooms upstairs. James's house sprung leaks in the dining room where water quietly but persistently trickled down a corner. He remained steadfastly cheerful and proclaimed that winter a fantastic adventure, as though we were all living out a modern-day version of *Little House on the Prairie*. He wasn't too far off in his thinking. Many friends in our circle were transplants from New York City or elsewhere and didn't have relatives nearby so we made families of ourselves and consoled each other with discussions of icicle lengths, pellet stove fuel, and cute pictures of our children inside the snow caves they dug in their yards. We took showers in each other's homes when the power went out and our children, with school cancelled for days, found new ways to play. One day when the roads were tolerable enough for a short excursion we took our son, who was six then, and one of his friends to an RV show in Hartford so they could marvel at the tiny bathrooms and scramble into the bunk beds and the little banquet tables. Darryl and I sat up front in the driver and passenger seats and dreamed of summer camping trips in 80-degree weather.

James managed to get the leak repaired and he remained cheerful. He napped on our couch while the kids played computer games and we watched the NFL playoffs on television. I felt inclined to follow his lead because the snow piled so high did make the world magical, and the drama kept the winter from being dark and boring. Plus I had the sense that it would all be done soon enough. I watched the calendar and put my faith in the sun's trajectory, refusing to believe the winter, as record-breaking and audacious as it was, would overstay its natural welcome. The days grew brighter on cue and the bite in the air lessened as February wore on. Sure enough, when the time came, winter let go of us and ushered in a fabulous spring with surprises of its own. A hydrangea in my yard that hadn't bloomed since I planted it there from a pot five years previously produced a wealth of blue flowers. I overheard gardeners at the nursery talking of the unusual health of their hydrangeas and out of curiosity I did an online search and discovered it was a boomer year for hydrangeas throughout the Northeast. No one seemed to know why. Perhaps it was our reward for enduring the harsh winter.

I probably would have accepted this gift without a thought and forgotten that winter except for those "Remember when?" conversations, but I still consider that winter now. In fact I ponder it endlessly because I eventually learned that while winter was letting go of us, James had been letting go as well. He committed suicide a few months later to our shock and grief. As we looked back, as all those left behind do, seeking signs or reasons or something to blame, my husband said he thought the winter somehow took too much out of James. I wondered if this was true. Was James a casualty uncounted? And could he move toward leaving us even as it seemed we all bonded more deeply as we weathered such conditions? What was breaking down in him even as we were coming together? It may seem unreasonable to hold a season accountable for a struggle James probably fought his whole lifetime without our knowledge, but a suicide leaves no ready cause, no one to blame, no matter how much we look to place both cause and blame. Still that winter, convenient and accessible, will just have to weather my grief and absorb my blame.

I think I loved winter once. Then I grew old enough to wield a snow shovel. Then my siblings and I would spend our days out there shoveling our long driveway. We also had to cut in a place for the mailman to get to the mailbox or else mail wouldn't be delivered—this could be disastrous. It was the only way my father could receive his Social Security checks. Rock salt came in red plastic bags. After moving to New England it took me a long time to trust the chemical ice melt products.

My father loved Christmas lights and I still would love to hear his thoughts on the current mania that has taken home displays to the level where homes have coordinated sound and laser shows programmed by computer and careful planning so they don't blow their fuse boxes. Careful upleveling through the years: It began with the requisite lights on the house lining the windows, doors, and framing. Then the Santa Claus, standing on the porch flanked by two plastic red candles topped with plastic yellow flame. They were heavy to maneuver out of the attic and onto the porch because he had poured sand into the bottoms of all three to keep the wind from blowing them over. Once at a garage sale he bought a little plastic pony, a child's toy, but he cut a hole into it, lit it up with a bulb, and put it on the porch next to Santa. Then came the Santa and sleigh with two reindeer mounted in the front yard, a rectangular patch of grass that went about one hundred yards from the house to the street. Once Daddy planted Santa there in the center it seemed obvious he should have lights all around him. So lights on the lilac bush, lights on the big boxwood, lights on the cherry trees, the plum tree, and the large Catalpa in the center. One of my brothers then had to scramble up the Catalpa and mount a star. The work was slow, my fingers freezing, and despite the results, I resented the effort. One year some teenagers pulled strings of lights off the trees and walked up the street breaking the bulbs. We found the detritus on the way to the bus stop. From then on Daddy made it impossible for them to do this again. He, or rather we, replaced the strings, but he had us secure the lines to the branches with thin pieces of copper wire that we twisted around the base of the bulbs as you would twist a tie to close a bag of bread. However, this couldn't be done wearing gloves so our job was made harder and colder. The wires scratched and poked my dry skin. It also lengthened the time it took to bring the lights down after the holidays. I hoped for storms then, hoping it would be impossible to take them down until the weather warmed up. But Daddy was adamant. The day after New Year's we would be out there taking it all down.

For all my complaining to myself, I loved those lights too. I would sneak out of the house after dark, especially if there had been a heavy snowfall, because it felt beautiful, safe. The color of each bulb shone through its cap of snow so what was white became red and orange, blue and green. Our yard was a patch of daylight in the darkness and I tiptoed in hushed wonder. It occurs to me now I should have been more concerned with footprints, that my father only had to glance through our front window in the morning to see someone had been out there. But then he probably noticed the size of the boot and realized it was one of us. He never said anything about it. Did he know one of his children wanted to conjure magic?

I think that memory is what I had in mind when, in October 2012, I signed up for a workshop, "The Soul of Winter," that I would attend as part of my ten-day January residency for the MFA program I was enrolled in at Vermont College. When I read the description of the workshop and how it would culminate in a three-hour solo meditation in the woods, my first instinct was to laugh and quote to myself my sister Jeanette's favorite saying: "See ya! Wouldn't wanna be ya!" By that time I had been cocooned, more or less, from the cold for at least eight winters because that's how long it had been since I lived in New York City where you walk everywhere and can't avoid firsthand encounters with the weather. In Connecticut I can get in my car, in the garage, drive somewhere, and only feel cold in the time it takes me to cross the parking lot and walk into a building. The time is lessened, of course, by how close I manage to park. Perhaps because of, not in spite of, this I couldn't dismiss the listing for "The Soul of Winter" entirely. I entered the program to challenge myself as a writer and I figured my issues with the season of winter might be a trial worth exploring.

So I made the decision to sign up for this workshop. It would take place at the end of December through early January. I considered my first pair of snowpants and bought double-layered mittens. I wondered what kind of boots would best protect my toes. I thought about taking walks in the morning cold to harden myself. I prayed and tried to sense my Source and feel at what point in winter I tend to lose hold of the line connecting us.

Then, on the morning of December 14, everything changed.

A nineteen-year-old boy, armed with warlike weaponry, blasted his way into my son's school, Sandy Hook Elementary. One of Tain's best friends, Ben, the youngest son of our close friends, David and Fran, was among the children killed. The event seemed to confirm my suspicion of God's absence and yet in every moment as the cold day unfolded, I knew the only way I would survive the ongoing aftermath is if I kept proving myself wrong. And this would be a tremendous necessity because in the days that followed I experienced a terrible duality in which I felt the situation demanded I marshal every strength of who I was while at the same time feeling dismantled on every level. And through this I somehow discovered winter held the clues for what I needed to be, and what I needed to become. In this gaping void I had to act out of faith and hope I would be answered. I remembered attending a party in a friend's home a few years ago and my friend's young son, a toddler, standing in the kitchen surrounded by all these tall adults like trees in a forest. Staring at all our legs at that level, he must have thought we looked the same. Still, he put his arms straight up, that's all he did. And I was struck by his utmost faith that someone would notice and pick him up. Because I was so moved by his action I wanted to be his answer. I went over to him and lifted him into my arms and waited for that look of, "Hey, you're not my mom!" But it never came. Having reached the high ground he sought, he looped one arm around my neck and calmly surveyed the room. In the crushing days after the shootings, when there seemed to be nothing but darkness, grief, and hordes of people and media, I wanted, needed, to be like that toddler. I wanted to reach out and feel in utmost faith I would be picked up and held by somebody so I could grasp a sense of myself again. But in the season when I am least connected to my God, when the worst had happened, how could I summon such faith again? Muscle memory or, perhaps more accurately, heart memory came into play. Acting on feelings and faith from the past would show me how to do this.

Then five days later I received an offer, one I didn't know I needed: Louise Crowley, the director of the writing program at VCFA suggested an escape, to come to Vermont early, before residency, with my family. It never occurred to me not to go to residency, which is amazing when I consider other times of grief— 9/11, the miscarriage of my first pregnancy—when I stopped writing for months. This tragedy knocked me every which way and still I was willing to put myself into community with other writers, most of them strangers. Perhaps this offer confirmed why. Among these strangers were many friends. More than friends, actually. I considered them my people, people it had taken me years to find.

When we arrived in Vermont a snowstorm blew up as though closing a door behind us when we took the exit for Montpelier. The room Louise had for us, a suite in the faculty dorm that looked out over the VCFA's main yard, was a perfect haven. We stayed indoors a whole day and watched through the windows as the flakes swirled around and made the campus seemed shaken in a snow globe. In that moment winter made sense. I felt hidden and safe. The next day Darryl took Tain sledding on one of the big hills in Hubbard Park. These slopes dwarfed ours in the local park at home so Tain was impressed. He also got to meet Ellen, my advisor from that semester, when she dropped by to check in on us. Tain lingered near the door when she was about to leave and I could tell he liked her. "I think he wants a hug," I told her and she happily obliged. Still, he told me it was nice here, but he didn't feel comfortable. "It's not like home," he said. I told him that was okay, but I was glad he would know where I would be for the next ten days. This made me feel better about their leaving after two days, which is when I moved into a regular student dorm room.

After I took them to the train station and parked my car in the campus lot, I decided I wanted to take a photo of College Hall for my Facebook page to establish my presence at residency. But I stood for a while, my booted feet buried in snow, staring at the building and not taking the picture. I realized I was looking at not the building but the thick black clouds behind it. Most of my classmates had not yet arrived so I was already feeling alone, out of place. I wasn't sure if I even wanted to see anyone and these clouds seemed to mirror my dark feeling. I didn't want to take a picture of such a sky. If I recorded this image I feared it would be sealed in me forever. I told myself to wait, that I didn't have to take the photo that day and residency would be long. Some light would come from somewhere. Just wait.

I went into my dorm, unpacked my belongings and sat on my bed but I felt conscious of my waiting. Out the window the clouds seemed to be shifting and I could see the faintest touch of blue sky. I thought perhaps I should go out to meet it, like Kate Winslet's Marianne from the film *Sense and Sensibility*: "There's some blue sky, let us chase it!" My plan was less energetic. I figured I would walk into town, get something to eat, and be alone for a bit. This might help me prepare to be among the other students when they came.

As I sat in the diner I realized I was looking for signs. I saw the golden brown onion rings of the young man at the counter two seats down from me and decided to order some of my own. When he was done eating I watched him roll a cigarette carefully with clean-nailed fingers and I wondered if I would get to see him light it and suddenly this hope of fire is very important. The cigarette is fatter at the end than at the part in his lips and it seems to me it would become a miniature torch if lit. But he leaves with the cigarette hanging unlit from his mouth.

When I finally leave the restaurant myself I looked to the west and I see light beginning to emerge. The gray shell of cloud cracked open and a line of liquid gold was spilling out along the horizon. I wondered if it would be fully open by the time I got back to campus.

I began the walk back up the hill. Midway through my climb I saw up and across the street a person coming down the hill dressed entirely in black and I could tell from the bouncy, purposeful way this person was walking that he or she was a sign. I started to feel an inevitability that I decided to take as hope. Then I realized the person is a friend, my friend Robert. As he waved and crossed the street to me I knew he had no idea what I was seeking and yet the bright, excited look on his face seemed to say, "Yes! I saw it! It's right back there at the top of the hill." Before we part he says I am walking the earth in a sacred manner. I find it interesting that he can see that, but then this is why we are friends. We see each other. The thought saddens me as well because the light of my friend should be enough and today it isn't. I need more and from a higher source. You would think I would run then, but I keep my slow pace, focusing on each step.

When I crest the hill and turn the corner there it is: the light greets me with golden glitter sprinkled upon the snow and College Hall framed in a blue sky dressed with puffy clouds. Even something about the blue is tinged with gold. I pull out my phone and take a picture then. This is the light I want imprinted in me. This is the light I want to keep. I think about how the blue sky when I see it like this seems to gaze back at me with the wonder of a child asking, "Why were you looking for me? I am always here, always, even if I'm sleeping beneath the clouds." It feels like a promise, a promise that will always be kept if I have faith and if I will wait.

As we begin our work in the Soul of Winter class we consider our attitudes toward winter, other artistic work. I thought about how winter takes on a different element when you must walk through it every day in a city like New York. I learned then the real difference between cold, freezing, and frigid temperatures. One morning I walked to the subway station, just two blocks from my apartment, and didn't understand why it hurt so much to breathe. Like it didn't matter that I was wearing a coat. Long coats for walking, short coats when I'm driving. Some people in the suburbs, I've noticed, rarely wear bulky coats because they are only going from their cars into a building. They will wear sweaters and vests and no more. This didn't occur to me until one winter I went to Ohio with my shearling and tried to get behind the wheel of a rental car while wearing it. Didn't work. Sometimes heavy is necessary. Walking through a wind tunnel between the buildings in midtown Manhattan, I'll take my shearling over a feather-stuffed parka any day of the week.

Our work is leading us to a vision quest of sorts. Over the week developed a plan to simply give myself time to grieve Ben— something I felt I'd had no time or room to do even slightly. I want the optimum level of connection so I fast, subsisting on juices and broth for two days leading up to the solo venture. From past experiences I know there is something about abstaining from food that gives me a clarity, a happy kind of energy that I somehow knew would be necessary if I was going to endure three straight hours of cold.

My solo sit began around 5:30 a.m. on a Sunday morning. I chose as my place a small clearance on the side of a mountain where I could see the lights of town from a distance. For the first forty-five minutes or so I did as little as possible. It's important to sit with darkness as long as possible—I learned this from a book, *The Dark Night of the Soul,* by a psychologist named Gerald May. He says it is in the darkness that God does his work with you, and we must not interfere or try to flee the dark. At one point I walked down the hill a ways toward the town and back up again to stay warm. As I turned to come back up I was stunned to see the darkness was even behind me because of massive black clouds in the skies right over my chair.

I was thinking of the dream I had of my father just before I woke up to come to the sit. Usually when I dream of my father I'm either telling him I miss him or I'm obediently listening to something he wants me to do. "Help your sister," he had said to me once in another dream. But in this dream my father was concerned because he seemed to know I was about to go on an uncharted journey—I was going somewhere without knowing where I was going. I smiled and even laughed at him as I told him it was okay. I could probably map it out with GPS if he wanted me to but he didn't find this funny. I said he wasn't being very helpful. "Helpful." He scorned the word as though it wasn't his job to be helpful.

Over my head, I saw birds flying. I wondered: is it their "dawn state?" Is it time for them to be?

I meditated—sometimes I silenced my mind, sometimes I found myself mentally listing gifts received and giving thanks for gifts of friendship, gifts of love and beauty, the gift of my child's life. I questioned what was next. I had come to the mountain with this idea in my head of having a kind of ceremony, my own burial of Ben. I have brought photos of him for this purpose, but I don't know when the process will occur. I sensed it wasn't time yet. I just kept in mind I had this work to do.

It was so dark I couldn't tell it was snowing. At first as I sat there I thought I had been careless with my clothes and bag when I see I have somehow managed to get snow all over myself. Then I realized it was snow accumulating on me. The soft tapping staccato notes I had been hearing were the flakes hitting my coat and snowpants.

At one point I stood and danced in the darkness. It felt like a continuation of my dancing at the graduation party the previous night. I heard the same music in my head. With all the clouds it was hard to tell day was coming on. I began to see it in the contrast of light between the sky above and the snow beneath me.

When my watch read 7 a.m. I decided to break my fast. I had not eaten solid food since dinner Thursday evening in preparation for this sit. I ate chunks of granola I bought at the farmers market the previous day for just this purpose. It was made with maple syrup, chocolate, peanut butter, almonds, walnuts, hazelnuts, and cinnamon. As I ate, I thought of how little Ben would not have been able to eat this snack. He had been severely allergic to nuts.

After I sat a little longer I decided it was time to begin the search for an appropriate burial spot. I walked a little ways down the mountain from my chair and I saw a single evergreen, like a little Christmas tree, with other tree stumps and saplings in front of it and hugging the side of the hill. As I looked at it I felt as though I could sense a child walking next to me. He was asking me for chocolate milk. He was asking me for cheese sticks even though his mother said he had eaten right before she dropped off him and his brother at my home. I could hear him in the woods behind my house with Tain. They were trying to figure out how to build a fort. I thought about the photo of me holding this child as a baby. I was crying then and I knew it was time. I went back to my seat and took out the three pictures of Ben. I felt impelled to write on them so I took out a pencil. On each one I wrote: *Benjamin Andrew Wheeler September 2006–December 14, 2012. I love you. Miss Fronie*

There was already a space beneath the tree because a bird had already dug in there to build its nest. I put Ben's pictures in the nest hole and covered them.

As I went back up the hill I noticed an odd streak of something in the snow near my chair. It was not quite light—it was a change of coloring, like it was about to be light. I looked up and saw a shifting in the sky and a fleeting patch of blue. I sat down and watched it. Then I saw a faint shaft of yellow and I realized, even though it was still snowing, the sun was about to come through. I changed the angle of my chair so I could face it. I propped my feet up on the snowdrifts in front of me. I began to sing the song our friends Mary and Kim sang at Ben's funeral by Ben's favorite band, the Beatles, "Here Comes the Sun." I especially liked singing the line "And I say, it's all right."

The sun did come through and in that moment I felt as though I was greeting a friend. The rest of the time on the mountain I was just sitting there with that friend as though we're together in front of a fire, even after the sun faded behind the clouds and I readjusted my chair to its original position overlooking the town. I sat there, my hood up, filled with this silence that wasn't really a silence. I was alone but not alone. It was familiar, like home. I was content to sit that way, my body curved around this warm pocket of being and in contemplation of this thing, the rest of the day.

Then I heard it—just once—so clearly, so matter of fact: "Sophfronia."

I turned in my chair. I don't know what I expected to see, I had only this sense that someone wanted me. I was so shocked to see three people, two teachers and a student, standing there. The sit was over. I felt interrupted, caught in the act even. But I know I also felt this churning excitement in my chest as I gathered my things and joined them. One of my friends smiled at me and it was as though he were saying, "Come on, Sophfronia! It's time for you to be!" I was so very happy to do so.

I learned later from Tim, the student standing with our teachers, that they had been standing there calling me repeatedly. "I don't think he was talking loudly enough," he said of Robert, the one who seemed most determined not to startle me. But then Robert is my friend and a close enough one that I'm sure he knew exactly who I was in communion with and had no desire to rip me from the nexus.

In fact I knew Robert could see it from the way he smiled at me as I joined them. Suddenly I really wanted to know what I looked like. This sense was so powerful that when I got back to the dorm I dropped my things and went straight into the bathroom to find the biggest mirror I could find. I just stood there and stared and I'm sure the women who walked through that morning must have thought I'd lost my mind. But I wanted to know exactly what I look like when I've been in the company of The One. I wanted to see my eyes the way my classmates saw them, when they said I was reflecting the light of the divine.

But then I could have just as easily been about to fall asleep. I could have been skirting an abyss and quiet ready, warm and content, to fall in and never resurface. I've heard you have a kind of delirium before you succumb to exposure. I could have died, just like the Little Match Girl. Was that what I was experiencing? My guess would be no—I wasn't cold, not even shivering.

Later I took a shower and changed clothes, but once I did I seemed woefully underdressed. I felt like I should look like a bride, in flowing fabrics of all colors. I felt like Rumi, like I'd been cavorting with the divine. It was so glorious. I didn't feel tired all day despite only getting about four hours of sleep the previous evening. I could have stayed up all night talking about this. I hadn't felt so "me" in such a long time. It was like, in the calling of my name, I had been recalled to life.

But what was so different for me? I was the same. I was not done grieving, as was apparent for me in the weeks and months to come. I did access something, something akin to joy. And it showed me it could sit and exist in this place even as I grieved, just as a little bird sitting in the snow with snow falling all around it. I did not have to be the either/or, comprising all grief, or displacing and forgetting the grief and being all joy. I would exist in both and it would be fine to exist in both. I didn't have to choose or try to be one or the other. And even all this I didn't have to understand completely.

PART FOUR

THE REALM OF SPIRIT BARE

THE HOLY WEEK WALK

*L*ent is supposed to be a time of darkness, but I had already
started off badly. Fasting, prayer, and alms-giving—I knew
these were supposed to be the focus of Lent so I had fasted.
For ten days after Ash Wednesday I did the Master Cleanse, but
it stripped my insides so clear that it awakened my body and my
mind to the point where I was seeing the world in glorious, high-
definition Technicolor. It generated an energy wave that I rode full
on into Holy Week. The day before Palm Sunday I was still glowing warm and happy like a newborn sun.

I spent most of that Saturday morning, a cold and rainy one,
in seminars at a local nursery. We all sat around a table in a
drafty barn with a concrete floor but I must have been radiating
heat because a cat named Coleus claimed my lap and purred and
snoozed there for over an hour. As the hydrangeas class began I
realized I had entered a full-blown state of gratitude. I'd recently
heard a lecture about this, about how gratitude, real gratitude,
can find you in the unlikeliest of circumstances and leave you
gob-smacked with awe and wonder. It's a feeling of wholeness

and an awareness of that wholeness in such a way that it brings utter joy. To me it's like what the boy Mickey sings in the Maurice Sendak children's book *In the Night Kitchen,* "I'm in the milk and the milk's in me. . . ." Everything is one. So in that moment I listened to the master gardener and felt as though he were sharing with me the secrets of the universe, like I had never been told before how to plant a shrub. He told me how I might get an oak leaf hydrangea to survive in my back flowerbed and I wanted to embrace him. I felt love, deep, deep, love—not necessarily for him but for the world.

That spring of 2012 was my second experience of Lent. I'd been baptized Episcopalian, along with my seven-year-old son, for only about six months then. Before coming to Trinity Episcopal Church I'd only thought of Lent, which I first heard of in college, as the time when my Catholic friend Eileen gave up chocolate for a few weeks. But my pastor explained you don't have to give up something—you can take on a practice as well. The point is to do something that can help strengthen your relationship with God and prepare you for Holy Week, another important time in the church calendar when we relive and remember Christ's passion: the journey into Jerusalem, the crucifixion, the resurrection. My first Holy Week was fascinating if only because it was a new practice for me to attend church every day for a week and participate in an all-night vigil on the night of Maundy Thursday. Last year I found myself singing when I didn't expect to, simply because I had been singing hymns every evening in church and the singing got infused into my being. But on another level that Holy Week felt like a blur because I was just trying to keep up with what was going on in the services: when to stand, when to kneel, when to light candles.

For my second Holy Week I was curious to see what would happen when I would be used to the activity of the services. I hoped to focus more on the words and the music, to walk the actual journey "from darkness to light" as it said in our church bulletin, and to walk it with open eyes, open heart, and open mind.

APRIL 1, PALM SUNDAY

As I drove my son to church that morning my concern was that the journey "from darkness to light" just couldn't happen. I was already so much in the light. The state of gratitude I felt at the nursery still flowed through me and around me. I saw light everywhere—in fact it streamed over my shoulder as the sun poured through a window above me as I stood in the lower level of our church, called the Undercroft, waiting for my son to don his choir robe. I told myself maybe this was not a bad or inappropriate way to begin Holy Week. After all it was the day we would "enter" Jerusalem waving the palms and singing "Hosanna!" It was supposed to be a joyous moment full of light and gratitude.

While I mulled over these thoughts my son Tain and his fellow Trinity Choristers emerged from the changing room and began surrounding our church's music minister as she passed out palm fronds. She looked like a Mother Goose in her black robe and long white cotta. The Choristers were her goslings waiting to be fed. Tain wore the all-black robe without the top because he was a novice. In June he would be "whited" and advance to wearing the cotta. I marveled at how quickly he had taken to the choir, how he had found his way into this new family.

Just over a year earlier he had asked me a question that signaled the start of all this for us. "Mama, what is Sunday School and can I go too?" He had been a fan of VeggieTales for months. It's an animated series, now all on DVD, of vegetables enacting their versions of Bible stories often with funny songs. Tain had been listening to the "Sunday School Songs" CD when he asked this question. "Yes!" I said without hesitation. "You can go! We'll all go!"

I had been hoping for just such a moment. I wanted us to be a church-going family, but I didn't want it to be something we did "just because it's Sunday" or "that's what this family does on Sunday." I wanted it to be my son's idea so he could own it, and feel comfortable knowing he was in a place where he could ask his questions about God, and have people who hopefully mirrored for him the same values we hoped to mirror for and instill in him ourselves.

But what church? Baptist was out of the question. The few times my parents had taken me to church I had disliked the cries and hollers of people getting the Holy Spirit. I wouldn't do that or subject my family to that. I had attended a friend's church but I could tell that, while friendly, its roots lay in the kind of funda-mentalism and Bible interpretation that I felt was too exclusive. And I just don't believe in the concept of hell—I wonder how people reconcile that thought: Yes, God is merciful and loving and forgiving but if you cross him or don't believe in him you get cast into a pit of fire. That makes no sense to me. Also the people of the congregation felt pained and needy, like I was in a hospi-tal. This alone wasn't a deal breaker because we are all broken and needy. But in that place it seemed there was too much focus on suffering and not enough on hope. I believe what Christ said about his coming into the world so we could have life in abun-dance. I wanted to be in a place that sensed the potential of such joy even if it wasn't there for everyone just yet.

My son had gone to an independent preschool housed in Trin-ity Episcopal Church, a huge gray stone church perched on top of a hill at the center of our town. I figured it was a space he was already comfortable with. Perhaps the religion would fit as well. One day I checked out the tracts, placed on small wooden shelves just inside Trinity's front door, explaining the faith. I learned the Episcopal Church is the American version of the Anglican Church. It held many similarities to the Catholic mass but with one big difference, as the comedian Robin Williams once pointed out: "You get all of the pageantry, none of the guilt." I liked the focus on community and acting out Christ's mission in true love and faith. The Episcopalian Church was not exclusive. This was the kind of structure I wanted for my son. As we came to know the people of the congregation, I knew this was the kind of com-munity I wanted for our family.

That Palm Sunday I was preparing to sit through the service by myself. My husband had attended the earlier service where he had sung with the adult choir.

"Who do you want to be?" Pastor Kathie approached me holding a handful of what looked like pamphlets. I knew these were the roles for the congregational reading of the Passion. "I've got Judas, Centurion, Servant Girl, High Priest, or Pilate."

I remembered last year thinking a person had to be in a community long enough to earn the privilege of doing things like readings, but Pastor Kathie was so casual about it. If something needed to be done she was always like, "Here, you can do it."

"I'll be Pilate," I said. "Last year I was Pilate's wife so I may as well keep it in the family."

This Passion reading was interesting to me because while you had the pastor at the podium reading the "Evangelist" or narrator role and someone else, this time a tenor up in the choir loft, reading the Jesus part, you had no idea who in the congregation would read the other roles. The voices seemed to come out of nowhere. So the girl who sat in front of me was probably shocked to find Pilate sitting behind her as I interrogated Jesus and offered up the choice of Barrabas.

Our worship services required a lot of two-track thinking and sometimes I found it frustrating. I would miss the beauty of one thing going on because I was so focused and committed to something else. I definitely didn't notice the practical movements of what went on at the altar. Recently, for instance, I received training in how to be an adult acolyte, namely, the one known as the crucifer, who holds a big golden cross and leads the processions at the beginning and end of the service. The guy training me asked if I had ever noticed how the crucifer and another acolyte come down and close the gates at the rails before communion. Well, no. I'm kneeling then and usually praying. When was I supposed to notice?

The previous week the music minister had visited the Lent class I attended on Wednesday afternoons with a handful of Trinity adults and did a brief lecture on the Holy Week services and the music featured in them. It really opened my ears. I'd never thought much about hymns other than to see how many verses we had to sing and when it would be over. The music minister explained how there are times when she chose a hymn because it had a really strong, emotional text. She showed us an example and said the choir would be singing this hymn, "Jesus Christ Our Lord," #458 in our hymnal, during Communion on Palm Sunday. She explained how she thought it would pair well with our reading of the Passion, because it told the story of the passion in the context of love.

> Here might I stay and sing,
>   no story so divine:
>   never was love, dear King,
>   never was grief like thine.
>   This is my friend,
>   in whose sweet praise
>   I all my days
>   could gladly spend.

I loved the words of this hymn and looked forward to hearing it on Palm Sunday. But my too-narrow mind entrapped me. I nearly missed the whole hymn because I was so focused on Communion. It wasn't until I had finished my prayer that I realized the choir was singing it and I managed to catch the last verse. I forgave myself for this, though, and at the end of the service I still felt light, hopeful, and happy—an auspicious beginning for my Holy Week.

APRIL 2, MONDAY

On this morning I walked a labyrinth for the first time in my life. At Trinity they lay out a labyrinth periodically throughout the year, but in Lent it is out every Monday and for Holy Week it stays all week. The labyrinth is painted on heavy canvas and is stored in sections. Jack, our sexton, has to take out all the pieces, roll them out on the Undercroft floor, and put them together, fastening each section with long strips of Velcro. He was still working on it when I first arrived so I went up to the sanctuary to sit and wait. I had expected to meditate and pray but as I sat there, taking in the quiet and studying the stained glass windows, tears

began to flow and slip down my cheeks. I cried. I cried a lot. I
don't usually cry and especially not like that, so I could only think
I hadn't done it in a long time and I must have really needed it,
especially since my mind was so full of all the work waiting for
me on my desk at home: my husband and I were in the process of
refinancing our mortgage, I needed to organize and file our taxes,
I had to design a workshop to sell and teach so we could have
an income over the summer when my husband's middle school
teacher paychecks stopped until fall. I could feel the glowing,
happy feeling of gratitude I had at the nursery slipping away even
as I checked my watch and wondered how much time I would
have to walk the labyrinth before I had to get back to my office at
home. Perhaps crying was my way of saying to the One, "Please
take this for a while."

When I left the sanctuary I saw Jack in the hall and he told
me the labyrinth was ready. In the Undercroft I admired it as I
removed my shoes. It was, and is, a beautiful thing. It's an octagon
of cream-colored canvas and the lines are painted dark indigo. Its
pattern is based on the labyrinth built into the floor of Amiens
Cathedral in France more than 800 years ago. On a table nearby
a set of fliers explained that the labyrinth "is one element in a
larger effort to encourage people to experience the rich depths of
spirituality found in Christianity." Many people mistakenly think
a labyrinth is the same as a maze, but a labyrinth is not a maze.
In a maze you can come to dead ends that require you to go back
and retrace your steps. In a labyrinth there are no blocked or
wrong paths—there's just one path in, and one path out, albeit
one full of twists and turns.

As I began my walk through the labyrinth I was surprised by
how tight and suppressed I felt in the early stages, especially on
the short parts and tight turns. I had to remind myself to breathe.
I took long deep breaths. Then for a bit it felt like a dance, like
the kind you see in a Jane Austen film. The paths became longer
and I felt myself expanding. There was more room as the paths
opened up and I felt like I wanted to run. *Stay. Stay here.* I kept
telling myself that to calm the feeling of the need for speed. I held
my arms and hands open at my sides so I might receive whatever
may come. Then I realized I had to quiet my mind because I heard

myself writing—I was conjuring words to describe the experience even as I walked. I had to bring myself back to the present again and again. When I reached the center of the labyrinth I sat down there and meditated. Finally everything went quiet then— my mind, my thoughts. Even the fan from the furnace turned itself off. When I finally stood again and began the walk back out through the labyrinth I could tell this time it felt different—I seemed to be taking the quiet back out with me. I was carrying it, cradling it like a sleeping child in my arms. All I could hear was this: something, was it my voice?—inside of me addressing the One, saying, *Walk with me. Walk with me.* And I kept hearing a response: *I am here. I am here.*

That same evening I attended the Taizè prayer service. It's form of group prayer modeled after a similar service done in the community of Taize in France. There's a small musical group, usually cello, violin, and flute that accompanies the congregation in a series of songs that are really meditative chants. One sentence or line is sung over and over. It is a comforting service. The lights are dim; the music is everything. We sing these brief pieces of music over and over and over again until it becomes a part of you. It is a way to pray constantly without realizing it. The composer Arvo Part has an album, *Alina,* and the simple piano and strings in that music stays with me the same way. I hear it even when I'm not listening to it and it provides a kind of stabilizing, comforting ribbon winding its way through my being.

I cried more tears—so many more tears. I began to weep the moment the music started. The *Ubi Caritas* was my favorite Taize chant/song: *Ubi caritas et amor, Ubi caritas, Deus ibi est.* It means, "Where charity and love are found, God himself is there."

That's a comforting, loving thought, but I didn't feel comforted. I felt like I was being dismantled, unmade, broken into little, little pieces. I was raw. The warmth I felt that rainy day at the nursery had dissipated. I felt cold. I kept my coat on and my hands in my pockets. My fingertips felt like ice. I wanted someone to come take my hand and warm it. But throughout all this I sang. I sang the chant over and over, opening up and pushing from my diaphragm and feeling the cleansing air go through me. Part of me wanted to ask, "What is this? What is this? Why do

I feel this way?" and I thought about the feelings I had over the weekend like that whole time was a dream I wanted to get back to. But the bigger part of me didn't want to question. I sat with it all as it was. I knew this would be the journey I was walking this week.

The service ended with a good long period of silence. It's a time, according to the program, when we were supposed to "continue to open our hearts to God," but I didn't know what was left to open. I felt like I'd already been sliced open through and through with a scalpel. At the end of the service I went into the chapel where Pastor Kathie was offering the laying on of hands and anointing for healing. As I knelt in front of her she whispered, "Anything specific?" meaning was there a particular thing or person I wanted the healing for. I said no and again the tears spilled down my face as she placed her hands on my head. She spoke a really long prayer for me that I didn't expect, and it included the words "let Sophfronia know that she is loved by You." She anointed my head with oil. I cried the whole time. I was touched that she prayed for me in this way because I had been thinking during the service that I tend not to ask for particular things when I pray. I'm of the mind that we are endeavoring to do things on our own. God doesn't take a stand, really, in giving us things, other than our talents, or making things happen. I'm not one of those people who thinks you can pray for your football team to win the big game. But what we can do is ask God to be with us and walk with us for guidance and strength as we try to figure it all out, while we try to accomplish what we want to do. In my prayer life I know that, in one way or another, I'm basically asking for the same things: *Help me to be open. Help me to trust the Divine and trust the path on which I've been set. Help me to see.*

I was exhausted when it was all over. On my way out of the sanctuary I looked for Rick, my friend who sponsored me for my baptism the previous year. He sang in the Taizè choir. In terms of spirituality, Rick is like having my own personal George Harrison. But in terms of looks and personality he's actually more like the actor Richard Belzer. He's got a head of thick, straight black hair peppered with gray. He was in a rock band in his youth and many days Rick threatens his wife that he will grow his hair long again. He is Italian, born in the Bronx. We are both Jets fans.

When I found him that night he asked me how I was and I said I couldn't seem to stop crying. He nodded knowingly. "It's always like this," he said. "I myself get very dark during Lent." Then he smiled brightly. "But you know it comes out good in the end!"

"Yes," I said and I laughed and he hugged me.

I couldn't believe it was only Monday. What would the rest of the week bring?

APRIL 3, TUESDAY

I attended Morning Prayer service at ten. It would be the only service for the day and it was very simple, just twenty-five minutes. I knew what to expect because I've done this particular office many times at home following along to a podcast that's broadcast daily from an Episcopalian priest in Maryland. It was all very familiar: the psalm, the readings, the Apostles' Creed, and the prayer of thanksgiving. Still, as I walked to my car afterward, I found myself in tears.

As much as this weeping bewildered me I was determined not to try to change my feelings. I wanted to sit with them and see where they took me. This meant I had to be careful with certain choices. That morning, for example, after I had taken my son to school and before going to church, I was in my kitchen getting ready to trim a pork shoulder to put in the slow cooker to make barbecued pulled pork for dinner. I stood there for a long time, though, before I got started because I couldn't decide what music to listen to while I worked. I didn't want to hear something too upbeat because I didn't want to manipulate my feelings. Sometimes I like listening to lectures but in the moment that didn't seem right either. I finally just put on one of my general playlists from my iPod. I heard a tune I hadn't listened to in awhile: "Color Blind" by Counting Crows. It is one of my favorites. The instrumentation is gorgeous: piano, cello, flute, and voice. That morning the lyrics seemed so appropriate, especially the line *pull me out from inside*. I most certainly felt turned inside out. And then there's this mantra-like part that I found comforting: *I am ready, I am ready, I am ready, I am fine.* I put the song on repeat and listened to it again and again for the next half hour while I worked on that pork shoulder.

APRIL 4, WEDNESDAY

The music minister had told our Lent class last week that many people despise Tenebrae, the Wednesday evening service, because it's very dark. Much of the text the lectors read for it is not Biblical. The word *Tenebrae* is Latin for "darkness" or "shadows."

But I wasn't thinking about darkness because, strangely enough, the sun had broken through that day, both literally and figuratively. Suddenly I had many things to be cheerful about: a dear friend had published a beautiful essay; the May issue of *O, The Oprah Magazine* with my picture on the contributors page arrived in the mail; I went to Lent class in the afternoon and had an invigorating discussion on many spiritual fronts, including what I'd been experiencing thus far in Holy Week. As I sat in my office I smelled the peanut butter toast my husband had made for an after-school snack for himself, and I could hear Tain coaxing him to give one of the slices to him. It was a "life is good" moment and I wondered how long it would last. Would my Tenebrae darkness be marred by these cheerful few hours?

It turned out I had underestimated Tenebrae. I had forgotten how long and dark the service was and wondered if I was experiencing a convenient amnesia—if I had remembered how long and dark Tenebrae was, would I have gone? I found my attention drifting and I wanted to fall asleep many times in the dim sanctuary. There was a set of fourteen candles in the altar area, and as we went through the night chanting psalms and hearing readings from Jeremiah, St. Augustine, and Hebrews, each candle was extinguished one by one. Toward the end came the eye-opening feature of the Tenebrae service: the loud sound signifying the earthquake that occurred after Christ's death. I had no idea who behind the scenes created the sound or how they did it. It sounded like a booming "Crack!" like a sledgehammer coming down on a concrete slab. It startled me even though I knew to expect it.

The service ended in silence and darkness. At the back of the church I received a quiet kiss on the cheek from Rick as I passed where he stood for his ushering duties. I went out into a cold and windy night. The sky was clear, the moon nearly full.

APRIL 5, MAUNDY THURSDAY

The foot washing of the Maundy Thursday service symbolizes the new commandment Christ gave to his disciples to love one another. He washed their feet before the Last Supper and we model this in the service to show both our love and our willingness to be loved. But all day as the time for the evening service approached I was thinking I would not take part in the foot washing. I was tired and feeling kind of prickly, like I didn't want to be touched. But I knew this was another part of the journey of Holy Week—to overcome the pockets of resistance within us. If I was serious about observing all that the week had to teach me, then I had to walk through this as well. When the time came I made myself get up from my seat to put my feet in the hands of a near-stranger. I received this bit of love, something I probably needed more than I realized.

The Maundy Thursday service ended in darkness as Pastor Kathie, Pastor John, and the acolytes stripped the altar. Tain had his head in my lap during all this and he was fast asleep by the time it was over. He went home with his father, but I stayed because I was taking part in the all night Watch in the chapel. Our church has a very monastic feel because it's so old. The chapel is tiny, and, at night, the space lit only by candles, you can almost feel the power of all the prayers that had ever been said in there. The Watch represented Christ's vigil in the Garden of Gethsemane. People signed up to cover the night in one-hour increments. I did the 10 to 11 p.m. hour. The previous year I did 1 to 2 a.m. and sat with someone who talked to me the whole hour. This night there were four other people in the chapel and we all read or meditated in silence. I was glad for the chance to sit. I prayed, meditated, and did some Bible reading—difficult to do because the only light was candlelight. During my meditation I nearly fell asleep and I kept thinking about the disciples who kept falling asleep in the garden. When I was a child I used to wonder why they could not stay up with Christ. As an adult I no longer wondered.

APRIL 6, GOOD FRIDAY

I attended the Stations of the Cross service in the afternoon. I'd never done this one before because last year I had been too tired but I'm glad I did it this time. I began a thought process that continued into the Good Friday liturgy, which I attended that night. I realized as I traveled through the Stations of the Cross that I had a problem with the story of the Crucifixion. I felt myself resisting it every step of the way. The violence of the story saddened me; the injustice overwhelmed me. I knew the necessity of it and I understood the insistence that this was done for me and the rest of the world, but I resisted it. As strange as this may sound, I knew what I had to do: I had to pull out my *Jesus of Nazareth* DVD.

This film, directed by Franco Zeferrelli, debuted as a television mini-series when I was about ten years old. It shaped much of my spiritual attitude. For some reason, and I can't remember when it started, I had a thing about watching movies about the life of Christ. Every time one came on, I watched it many times over: *The Greatest Story Ever Told, King of Kings,* you name it, I saw it. I had been a questioning child and, being a visual learner, these movies were my way of finding answers. When *Jesus of Nazareth* first aired I could tell even then that it was different from all the other films I'd seen. The teaching, the way people reacted to Jesus, was very *real life.*

Here's what I mean: in a film like *The Greatest Story Ever Told,* it seemed like Jesus only had to walk past a disciple and the guy would just drop everything and follow Jesus as though he were in a trance. Even as a child I could see that didn't seem plausible. But in *Jesus of Nazareth* I saw the struggle Peter and the others had in deciding to follow Christ. At one point Peter even said to the other disciples, "Why did you bring him to me? This is my life—my fishing nets, my family." Another time he said, "I'm just a stupid man." This film touched me profoundly, especially the scenes where Jesus taught of love and the love God has for us. There's a beautiful scene with Christ, played by the British actor Robert Powell, and Nicodemus, played by Laurence Olivier, that enacts the "born again" conversation that I just love. Nicodemus later told the other leaders of the temple that, in hearing Jesus speak, he felt "lifted out of himself" and felt "very aware of God being with us." I feel this way too every time I watch this film.

But here's the thing: because I was so touched by the love in this movie, it made the crucifixion scenes that much more terrible to take. I even had a hard time with the scenes after the resurrection, because Christ is sitting with the disciples and one of them is pleading him to stay with them because the day was nearly done and night was coming. And even though Christ tells them not to worry, that he will be with them until the end of time, it still saddened me greatly. Now as an adult, with first a video and then a DVD player, I had for years exercised the power of the remote control. I had stopped watching the end of the movie, including the crucifixion. I realized if I was going to take in the fullness of the journey of Holy Week I had to go back to that part of the story.

APRIL 7, HOLY SATURDAY

I was looking forward to the Great Vigil of Easter, but it didn't go well. I had Tain with me and the service was really late, 8 to 10 p.m. We had planned to leave early because, as a chorister, Tain had to be up early for Easter service. However, I thought we would at least get to the part where they turned all the lights in the church back on, proclaimed the risen Christ, and we would ring bells and use all sorts of other noisemakers. I had brought a bell and Tain had a kazoo. He was fascinated with the church being in complete darkness when we began until Pastor Kathie lit the Paschal flame. From that flame all the candles in the church were lit, including candles we were supposed to hold throughout the service.

This felt like the never-ending service, though. The lectors recite long readings starting with the beginning of Genesis. We had heard only the first reading before Tain began to complain. He gave me his candle when he was tired of holding it and I tried unsuccessfully to balance it with my candle while following along in the program. But when the burning candles spilled over and I got hot wax on my hands I knew it was time to go. I was disappointed and feeling tired and put upon. I'd had no chance to sit or pray or think about anything. But, to be honest, I'm not sure if I could have done so even if Tain weren't there. I didn't feel connected to all of those readings, all of those words on the page.

After I got home and put Tain to bed (Darryl was singing in the choir so he was still at church), I fired up the DVD player and watched the last hour of *Jesus of Nazareth*. Here, finally, through the miracle of the television ether and the talent of a bunch of actors, some now long dead, I found the connection I had been seeking. I cried during the crucifixion scene, cried even harder when Christ's mother Mary took up his dead body in her arms. How many times had she done that motion when he was a child, picking him up with her hands under his arms like I had just done that night for Tain when I carried him up to bed? Mary Magdalene is in this scene also and she kisses his feet. MM is played by Anne Bancroft and when I think of the story of the Passion, especially the way it is played in this movie, I have always felt I was most like her. When Christ was still on the cross, his mother and Martha were being allowed by the Romans to go past the guards to stand directly beneath him. Mary Magdalene sees them going and she kind of sneaks past the guards to join them. When a centurion stops her she says, "Please, I'm with the family." The centurion asks Mary and Martha, "Is that right?" and they both look at this strange woman they don't know, but they tell the guard, "Yes." So MM gets in there, she finds a way to be close and show her love. So it makes perfect sense that she is there to help anoint the body and discover Jesus is gone from the tomb. Later, when she tells the story of seeing the risen Christ, I love the part where she says, "And then he said my name—'Mary.'"

I don't like the feeling of being powerless to do anything about Christ's death. I know I'm not supposed to do anything—it was meant to happen. It's a ridiculous and maybe even egotistical feeling I have and yet I want to be MM and *do something* and *feel something*, although I don't know what. I just want to get in there, at the foot of the cross, and *be* there, like she was. What is the equivalent of that now?

APRIL 8, EASTER SUNDAY

Pastor Kathie delivered a sermon that sounded like she'd heard my queries. She said there are some spiritual journeys that are intellectual, based on doctrine, while others are visceral, emotional, personal, and real. Had I been seeking the visceral and emotional? Was this why I wanted to see *Jesus of Nazareth,* because so much of what I'd been doing was too intellectual? Kathie even talked about what I had noticed in the film about the calling of Mary Magdalene by her name. In saying her name, the risen Christ gives Mary that visceral experience, that sense of being known and recognized. Kathie said we long to be known by God, not as part of some grand connection to the cosmos, but as who we are as individuals in our lives and in our bodies. His grace travels to the most personal space in us, she said, engaging all our senses, and this is invoked by the speaking of our name.

But my most profound experiences with God have always been visceral, very much like the feelings I had at the nursery. What is gratitude, after all, if not an overflowing recognition of God's grace? I think in making the journey of church, like this Holy Week, I was trying to find an intellectual basis to some how "catch up" with the visceral; that the doctrinal would help me make sense of the visceral. Maybe I needed to let go of some of the doctrinal, and perhaps my church bulletin too, and stick with the visceral.

This might be my continuing journey—to place the visceral/emotional/personal front and center and allow the communal experience of church to feed that feeling. I could take inspiration from texts and from the words of others like Pastor Kathie's when such words come my way. But I would seek to feel both the light and love I felt at the nursery in balance with the tears and longing that emerged as Holy Week went on. Perhaps light and the longing are the same, a reaching from within me desiring the fulfilling presence of my God; to be here, living gloriously in the fray of life's abundance and hoping forever to hear, *I am with you always.*

WHY I MUST DANCE LIKE
TONY MANERO

I've got the DVD of *Saturday Night Fever* playing in my writing studio—again. I don't mind putting on a beloved film or television show and letting it run over and over to keep the house from being too quiet when I'm working alone. It's a habit that drives my husband crazy. "You watching this again?" he'll ask when he comes home at the end of the day to find me throwing myself around the room in my freestyle interpretation of the tango hustle. But today I'm neither dancing nor ignoring the film. I'm really watching it. I sit silent, engrossed. I have my tools—paper, pen, and, in my mind, a collection of thoughts and memories—around me. I'm trying to excavate or isolate something I've recently discovered in *Saturday Night Fever*. It's there in words, yes, but it's also a feeling or a kind of inspiration, and that makes it harder grasp, hence this particular intense viewing. It's something about the character of Tony Manero that tells me something about myself. I am trying to listen.

When I usually have this movie on I pay attention only at the good parts and those, of course, in *Saturday Night Fever,* are the dance scenes. So often I'm not watching as Tony, portrayed by the John Travolta I had a mad crush on when I was ten years old, goes on his famous strut through Brooklyn. I'm not looking when he orders the two slices of pizza, stacks them on top of each other, and shoves half of the mess in his mouth, getting sauce on his idyllic chiseled face. And when he and his friends walk around their neighborhood spouting their litanies of oversexed, racist, ignorant, misogynistic remarks I ignore them. I don't want to hang out with those guys. One day, though, during the neighborhood scene with his friends, I happened to glance up from my computer and glimpsed a look on Tony's face that seemed to agree with me: He didn't want to hang out with these guys either. I'd never noticed it before.

I grabbed the remote and backed up the DVD. When I watched the scene again I heard a line that, in Tony's own way, confirmed what I saw. "This is bullshit," he says to his friends, but they have no idea what's bugging him. He seems restless, frustrated, dissatisfied. I saw the inkling of something big—Tony was getting a sense that there was something very small about his way of life. I started the film from the beginning. I wanted to see if this look showed up anywhere else, and it does. I never realized how many times, in that first scene at the disco, Tony's friends offer him drugs and he turns them down. "Can't you guys get high enough from dancing?" All he seems to want is the time, money, and space to do the only thing that doesn't disappoint him: dancing. And before I could even ask myself why, I heard with new ears and empathy his dialogue with Stephanie, the girl he wants for a new dance partner, about how the only time he feels a real high is when he's dancing.

"I would like to get that high someplace else in my life," he says.

"Like where?"

"I don't know, some place, I don't know. Dancing, it can't last forever. It's a short-lived kind of thing. But I'm gettin' older, you know? I feel like, so what, I'm gettin' older. Does that mean I can't feel that way about nothin' left in my life? Is that it?"

I'm watching *Saturday Night Fever* again because I know Tony's yearning is the same as mine. The more Tony dances, the more alive he feels, and yet this awakened state makes him more dissatisfied with his lot. He knows there's supposed to be more: more good energy, more good feeling, *more life*. "How come we never talk about how we feel when we're dancing?" he asks. Good question.

I want to tell him, "Come hang out with me and Lucy. We can discuss it for days." Lucy is Lucy Honeychurch from another of my favorite movies, *A Room With a View*. I first saw this film version of the E. M. Forster novel when I was in college and while I loved everything about it—the gorgeous scenery, the period costumes, the wildly romantic kiss George Emerson plants on Lucy in an Italian field—what stayed with me the most—in fact it drove me to read the book—was the scene in which Lucy, portrayed by Helena Bonham-Carter, passionately plays the piano in the lobby of the *pensione* in Florence. Afterward she is uncomfortable, restless—dissatisfied. This leads the vicar listening to her to comment on how he would make her a heroine in a novel.

"And I should write, 'If Miss Honeychurch ever takes to live as she plays, it will be very exciting, both for us and for her.'"

Lucy replies, "Mother doesn't like me playing Beethoven. She says I'm always peevish afterwards."

Peevish? Why peevish? It seemed a silly word masking something more important—and familiar—to me. When I got to this same section in the novel, I found myself whispering, "Yes. True, of course," over and over again. Performing Beethoven so expands Lucy's world—shows her the possibility of more life—that she is peevish and frustrated when the piece is over and her life, her world, is still as small as it ever was.

"Lucy never knew her desires so clearly as after music," Forster wrote. ". . . the gates of liberty seemed still unopened. She was conscious of her discontent; it was new to her to be conscious of it. 'The world,' she thought, 'is certainly full of beautiful things, if only I could come across them.' It was not surprising that Mrs. Honeychurch disapproved of music, declaring that it always left her daughter peevish, unpractical, and touchy."

I have known this about Lucy for years, but Tony Manero has awakened me to her anew, making us a strange triangle of kindred spirits: a girl from Edwardian England, a boy from 1970s Brooklyn, and a modern-day Connecticut mom. I suppose I've recognized the pilgrim souls in all of us and I'm trying to chart my journey by their footprints. I think we're connecting now because, having survived the semi-conscious sensory overload of my twenties and thirties, I have grown quiet enough to notice the moments of energy that drive me. I know what it feels like to have the high Tony talks about. Now my question is the same as his: where can I get that high? Or, and perhaps this is a better, more accessible query, how can I live a life that will allow me to encounter the "beautiful things" Lucy speaks of?

I sense the answer coming closer as I get older, only it's not a singular, corpulent thing I can reach out and grasp like a piece of ripe fruit. It's something like a deep swath of river I must step into, up to my neck if necessary, so I can feel how it lives and flows around me. I want to be so steeped in Tony's kind of high that I don't ever feel like I'm living life in miniature. I know it's not possible to exist in this state constantly, but I'd like to think I can cultivate my days so I always have a chance at least to encounter the transcendent moments that take me beyond myself. Such an endeavor is ambitious, yes, but I've come to an age where I see how much it matters, how it may even be all that matters.

Where do I need to focus most when I consider this way of living? I'm putting aside for the time being my roles as wife and mother. Let's say it's a given I will always, if I remain as fortunate as I've been in these areas, receive a certain measure of love, energy, and emotional support on the domestic front. For now I'm considering the rest of me, stripped to my essence and seeking to understand what feeds, inspires, and motivates me at my core. I think it comes down to my physical, artistic, and spiritual/emotional being.

What I believe about these three areas takes me beyond the usual considerations. For instance, in terms of my physique I do exercise and watch my weight, but not because I feel compelled to look as I did in college or run a marathon in the near future. I just want to be ready—ready for an opportunity to experience my physical being in different ways. Like the time last spring when our pastor's husband, Shep, posted on Facebook that his daughter could not accompany him for a big charity motorcycle ride. Did anyone want to replace her? I said yes without thinking. I'd never been on a motorcycle yet there I was the next morning shmushing a helmet the size of a small microwave oven down over my head. I wondered if it were possible to develop claustrophobia. The helmet featured a built-in microphone, and Shep showed me how to plug it into the motorcycle's electrical system. He would do the same with his helmet so we could talk to each other during the ride. This turned out to be really important. We rode with 3,000 participants and the accompanying roar of their motorcycles. At times Shep would ask "Are you all right back there?" but other times he would say, "I'm going to stand up for a moment" and pop right up out of his seat. If he had done that unannounced I probably would have screamed loud enough to knock us both off the bike.

The route we followed is a favorite of mine: CT-34, a twisting road that meanders before crossing, in a narrow passageway, over the Stevenson Dam, which corrals the Housatonic River to form Lake Zoar. I often drive it in the mornings, and I love how the road goes east, into the sun. The light bathes the water and the riverside homes in a beatific glow, and at times I see the Yale crew team, rowing archangels, working diligently toward home. But it's hard to watch the river and appreciate its curves while keeping my eyes on the road. On the back of the motorcycle I didn't have to worry about steering, and I was so close to the road it felt like I was holding hands with the river and running, running along with it as it flowed through the land.

I wore a Canon SLR, its strap wrapped around my body. I quickly realized I didn't have to hold on like I'd seen in movies, women on the backs of motorcycles, their arms welded in circles around the waists of men wearing sunglasses but not helmets. So I took pictures, even daring to lean out and turn back and shoot behind us. I pretended I was a Tour de France photographer on the back of a motorbike zooming through quaint French streets and up into the Pyrenees. I found I was comfortable leaning into the turns, trusting the angle of the motorcycle and its momentum as we curved toward the earth before bearing up again. Throughout the ride I flipped up my visor more than I should—I didn't want the tinted plastic between me and the hopeful light green color of new leaves in the trees over our heads, no matter how windblown and dry my eyes became. We arrived at a mall in

Trumbull about two hours later and I was so famished I sucked
down a McDonald's smoothie with a cheeseburger because that
was our best option with all the riders swarming the food court
but I didn't care. I felt strong and whole.

When I got home that evening my first impulse was to lie on
my back on my bedroom floor, as I would do at the end of a
yoga class, so my body could settle and integrate the day's energy.
How do I describe such energy? I suppose it's like, as Dylan
Thomas describes it, "the force that through the green fuse drives
the flower." It's not just a burst of energy spent quickly—this is
energy seeking to form, to create, to replicate. It is pushing me
open as a bud blossoms.

As a writer and reader I am seeking this energy in the form of
what I'll call the gorgeous risk. In the same way a dancer like
Mikhail Baryshnikov or even Tony Manero can make me rethink
how a human body can move, the gorgeous risk is the way a work
can inspire me to view beauty and truth in new and challenging
ways. That may seem vague, but I know what it sounds like when
I hear it. Recently I attended a reading where a writer presented
a kind of experimental essay. I know the piece was successful, but
I can't tell you if it was because of its structure or the lyricism
of its prose poem form. To be honest, I really can't tell you what
exactly happened in the writing because I was too caught up trying to absorb the massive energy of it. It was fantastic, this piece.
It was so full of risk and emotion and splendor—the energy rang
through the air and flooded the room. I wanted to run. I wanted
to stay. What the writer read was so beautiful and so true it hurt
and the pain was exquisite. I wanted to put my hands over my
ears and I wanted to stomp my foot and plead for him to stop.
I was watching him going out on the high wire and I wanted to
scream, "Oh my God, stop, stop! Someone is going to get hurt!"
But at the same time I couldn't stop watching and I couldn't stop
listening because that was exactly where that writer wanted to
be—taking that risk, living that risk. He knew the only way to do
it would be to go out on the wire because that's the only way to
get to the light at the other side. And that's also why I couldn't

stop listening—because I want to go there too. I'm talking about risk, but I should point out that what this writer read wasn't any sort of graphic, spill-guts-on-the-page, tell-all prose. Yet it was filled with his simple, emotional truths such as a touching, one-sentence description of the way his wife laughed. He layered these truths, one upon the other, until suddenly he'd made this complex creation reminding me of something so easy to forget in everyday life—that the little loves do matter; the way we notice a laugh or a butterfly on a sprig of lilac that make us who we are as artists and differentiate what we have to bring to the page.

After the reading I walked out of the building and nearly fell down the front steps. Every muscle in my legs trembled and as much as I wanted to seem calm and cool too, my body told me otherwise. Like Lucy Honeychurch I could barely stand to hear anything else or listen to another writer read for the rest of the day. Hearing and feeling so much risk had made me hyper-aware when the risk was absent. I was impatient and peevish. I knew I wasn't giving other writers their fair due. They too were writing their own truths, on their own paths. But this is how I was that day. The world felt too small.

This is what Adam Zagajewski is writing about, I think, in his book of essays *Another Beauty* when he says, "Anyone who's ever been deeply engaged in works of the imagination will know what I have in mind: that moment when, after a long period of immersion, we suddenly bob to the surface and find ourselves stranded in a kind of no-man's land. The friendly, ardent flames of imagination have abandoned us, but we don't yet stand on the solid ground of everyday common sense. We're suspended for an instant between two spheres that probably converge at some point, but we have no idea where (not in us and not for us). It's a treacherous moment; anyone who starts making lunch or dinner at such a time must take care not to precipitate a fire or even an earthquake."

I am trying to define this no man's land so I may pound in stakes and find the convergence; make a home here if that's at all possible.

My spiritual and emotional beings—I consider them connected because I think I have to be strong in spirit in order to love in the way I aspire to. There's a Lakota prayer that says:

Wakan Tanka, Great Mystery, teach me how to trust
my heart, my mind, my intuition, my inner knowing,
the senses of my body, the blessings of my spirit.
Teach me to trust these things
so that I may enter my Sacred Space
and love beyond my fear,
and thus Walk in Balance
with the passing of each glorious Sun.

The prayer, as I found it printed in a bulletin at my church, came with an explanation that according to the Lakota, the Sacred Space is the space between exhalation and inhalation. To "Walk in Balance" is to keep Heaven (spirituality) and Earth (physicality) in Harmony. I like the phrase "love beyond my fear," I feel potential there—potential for the same kind of energy that comes from the dance floor or the motorcycle seat. When I speak of love I'm referring to my friends, people I have no reason to love but I do because they managed to capture some part of my heart for their own. This risk here is in leaving space for new connections to develop. I'm not interested in having thousands of Facebook friends, but I do want the right friends close to me. I am, as Emily Dickinson might put it, a soul seeking my society. This is perhaps the greatest risk I take because the potential for pain is always present. To have a heart so open is to, as Annie Dillard puts it, "reel out love's long line alone, stripped like a live wire loosing its sparks to a cloud, like a live wire loosed in space to longing and grief everlasting." The longing and the grief parts do give me pause—they come because even if a friendship doesn't work out, and I've experienced a few of these, I tend to still love the person. I don't believe in hitting the delete button in my address book when a real affection exists, even if it's one-sided. I feel the challenge to love this way is a worthy one.

In the Martin Scorsese documentary *George Harrison: Living in the Material World,* I was struck by the depth of emotion the ex-Beatle's many friends displayed when speaking of him. By the time of the filming, Harrison had been dead seven or eight years and still these people—comedian Eric Idle, artist Klaus Voorman, and race-car driver Jackie Stewart among them—visibly mourned. Finally, an interviewer asked Idle, "What do you miss about him?" His answer: "I miss the way he loved me." I never heard a man describe a friend like that before. I wanted to cry because these friends weren't talking about Harrison's music, or his time with the Beatles, or the way he intervened for Bangladesh, or helped Idle and his Monty Python troupe finance the film *Life of Brian*—they missed the way he cared about them, the way he sincerely wanted to know what was in their hearts. That is the way to live—and love, I thought.

I find the best way for me to love this way is be as fearless as I can. I don't tiptoe around with niceties hoping I don't offend or scare anyone. If I love a friend, male or female, I will say so. As I grow in this, I'm more of the mind that it's never a bad thing to hear someone loves you—for certain of my friends I think it's even a soul-soothing necessity. It does make a difference—and I do mean the most essential, gob-smacking, head-turning difference. When one of my friendships has blossomed into this kind of deep loyalty and intimacy, my friend and I can spend hours in each other's company without realizing such time has passed. I have wandered away many afternoons in Central Park with my friend Jy, discussed foreign films and books for hours with Maria, sat by a river all morning with David, taken long walks to talk writing with Peter. I just go with it, and that means, right now, not making excuses each time a friend comes to mind and I want to call or send an email. I'm learning to step over such thoughts like a fallen tree in my path. I send the email. I pick up the phone. I write the letter. I'm surprised by how exhilarated I feel after I connect with a loved one.

That seems to be what I'm learning here—whenever I make a move whether it be trying a physical feat, writing a challenging new piece, or saying, "I love you," the energy is always there. If I want to partake of it I must trust, step out into the air, and wait for the miracle to make its move too. I've been reading Thomas Merton's *The Seven Storey Mountain,* and at times I marveled at his ebullient praise of the saints and his complete embrace of the Holy Virgin Mary. This person, who once considered himself an atheist, didn't just convert. He jumped out there, fully in love, placing his heart into something he could barely understand, moving toward it mainly based on the feeling that what he was feeling felt like life to him. Everything he did before that only reflected death back to him in the form of illness and oblivion. I know I want what feels like life to me—I'm seeking adventure in the lines of a poem, cooking for my family in my kitchen, warming my face in the laughter of a friend, even if that laughter comes because my friend has stumbled upon me dancing the tango hustle with Tony Manero.

SPIRITUAL JOURNEY
MILE MARKER

ROB BELL, NYC

What is a spiritual journey? On some days it feels like I'm on a bus like the one in the film *Almost Famous*, and my mates and I are zooming down the road singing Elton John's "Tiny Dancer" at the top of our lungs. Cool like that. But it can also take on the dreariness of the Beatles' bus in the film *Magical Mystery Tour*, a ride full of colorful people tooling down the road waiting to see what would happen. Only nothing much did.

Most of the time, though, on my journey I'm in my car alone and I'm thinking—and I'm praying. I am seeking. What am I seeking? To strengthen my relationship with Christ and, through Him, God. As the song "Day by Day" from the musical *Godspell* goes, *To see thee more clearly / Love thee more dearly / Follow thee more nearly, day by day.*

There are times like now when I know I'm on the verge of something that will take me deeper in this quest. But I don't know what it is, or even if my thoughts make sense. I contemplate it over and over. I think it has something to do with understanding a way of being. I've been coming to the realization that my "job" is to be Sophfronia, and this job requires me to discern in any given moment what that means. *What is happening in this situation? Is there work here that is uniquely mine to do?* But I wonder—are such considerations too self-centered? Especially when I feel these thoughts draw me ever inward. My profoundest experience of God is a personal one and when I sense His love during these ruminations I want nothing more than to withdraw, be alone, and contemplate that love.

And yet this doesn't feel quite right either. I don't think I'm supposed to be some kind of hermit or contemplative. Because I feel an outward tug as well, something pulling me out into the world. What's going on here?

I'm not sure. So at this point in my spiritual journey I've been driving around a roundabout. I keep going around and around because I don't know which exit to take. It would help to have signposts offering suggestions and direction. *Turn here. Try this route and see what happens. What if you simply stopped now?*

That's where Rob Bell comes in. I stopped at the Rob Bell mile marker.

Who is Rob Bell? On his website his bio simply describes him as "a bestselling author, international teacher, and highly sought after public speaker." He is all of those things, but it's a bit more complicated than that.

He was the pastor and founder of Mars Hill Bible Church, a Michigan-based congregation that grew to 10,000 members under his leadership. He wrote popular books and was featured in a series of short films called NOOMA that, according to the product description, "explore our world from a perspective of Jesus." In 2011 *Time* magazine listed Bell among its 100 Most Influential People. The same year he published his book *Love Wins: A Book About Heaven, Hell, and the Fate of Every Person Who Ever Lived,* which challenged, as noted in the *New York Times,* "traditional Christian views of heaven, hell and eternal damnation." It met with a maelstrom of criticism from evangelical Christians labeling Bell a heretic. Not long after this he left Mars Hill to pursue a different path of teaching and new ways of thinking about the word "church."

I first encountered him in a Christian formation class at our church watching the NOOMA film entitled *Name.* Since I'm graced with the unusual moniker of Sophfronia issues of name and identity, as you can imagine, are frequently on my mind. In the film Bell asked how much of our pain comes from not knowing the answer to the question "Who are you?" We shouldn't be afraid to dig and not only find the answer, but also live the answer. "Jesus invites us to be our true selves," he said. His words intrigued me. I was also enthralled with what I call the "may you" messages he delivers at the end of all the NOOMA films. To me the phrase "may you" is a high form of blessing, calling you to a higher form of yourself. For example, at the end of *Name,* Bell said,

> *May you do the hard work of the soul, to discover your true self. May you find your unique path, the one God has for you, and in the process may you find yourself comfortable in your own skin.*

Yes.

Bell hit a new level of popularity when Oprah Winfrey tapped him to discuss his book *What We Talk About When We Talk About God* on her television show, then included him on her 2014 Life You Want speaking tour. At this point he also met with a new level of backlash, and weathered complaints he had abandoned the church for some vague kind of new age spirituality.

To be honest, I paid little attention to the brouhaha. As a former journalist I've observed enough backlashes to know that when these things dust up, it has little to do with the person and a lot to do with others (institutions and individuals) serving their own interests, usually to attract publicity, at the person's expense. But I can't parse out the motives of others. All I can do is ask myself the question "What is this person saying and does it speak to me?"

When it comes to Rob Bell the answer is and continues to be, "yes."

From all I've read and from all I've sensed about him, my gut tells me this: he believes what I believe, and we go about our faith in a similar way. He is one of my people.

Notice I don't say I am one of his people. My spiritual journey is not about following gurus or cults of personality. It is about connection—finding friends, kindred spirits, brothers and sisters. Once encountered, we tend to recognize each other.

In fact I felt an inevitability when a parishioner at my church sent the email saying Rob Bell would be speaking near us, at the Town Hall in New York City, and offering to order the tickets so a group of us could attend and sit together. It seemed it was time for me to see him in person.

Bell's presentation, "Everything Is Spiritual," is essentially a long-form riff developing toward a new parable—a story that offers a different way of looking at ourselves and of wrestling with our rational minds. He used a whiteboard in the shape of a flat megaphone—a prop I found amusing and appropriate because in smile, height, and demeanor he reminded me of the male cheerleaders among my college classmates. And his message was a kind of extended, high-energy declaration. He drew a dot on the smallest end of the whiteboard, labeled it PARTICLE, and proceeded to tell us the story of expanding matter of the universe, from particles to atoms, to molecules, to cells, and how all this culminated in our place as humans in this miraculous happening.

And even if you don't believe in God, he noted, it must be acknowledged something amazing is going on. There is something divine about our design. On a certain level we are, he said, "finely calibrated arrangements of stardust," and yet we can dream, have compassion, we can love. "Your soul can soar," he said. "You are an exotic cocktail . . . an epi-phenomenon."

Yes, I could agree with that. I've always believed in the T-shirt motto "God Don't Make No Junk." I have an outsized belief in my specialness, something I've had since I was a child, and I know it can even be unsettling. It is the foundation of this sense I have of my "job" to be Sophfronia. I know I am a beloved child of God.

But in listening to Bell talk about molecules and stardust and dark matter, I began to think he would take me no further along in this rumination. I thought what he was saying was intriguing and interesting. Yes, it's great we're all here, we're fabulous, conscious beings on some unknown trajectory. But are we all on this trajectory as solitary individuals? It seemed that way. I admit I was thinking, "Does Rob Bell have something to tell me? No. Not tonight."

Then, as though he'd heard my thought, Bell began to address the "what's next." He drew several stick figures at the wide end of the whiteboard and talked about community, about vocation, about connection—topics so much on my mind I'd been discussing them with a friend that same afternoon. It was as though Bell had been sitting there with us at my friend's table the whole time.

He explained how it is possible that as we expand and grow (and by "we" he means not just people but the very essence of what we are on a subatomic level, the whole being of existence and matter as it were) we come to a point where we are not being pulled apart, but pulled together. "Human beings bonding with others of similar essence and substance" is what he called it. It is the next level. "Is there something we are being pulled together to form?" This of course could be another way of thinking about the Body of Christ and "an energy both universal and personal surging through us."

This would explain the outward pull I feel. He said it is a natural progression, even necessary. Let's go back to that thought about my "job." I am a writer and I come to my desk each day hoping that something I write will serve others. It is my vocation. But this "being Sophfronia" I think is my greater "work" in that it communicates I am a beloved child of God. It is of utmost importance to my soul that I understand and believe this. And in his discussion of how we are drawn together Bell affirmed for me the what and the why of this position: When I carry myself with the spirit and confidence that comes from being beloved—and this also goes for any well-loved child—it does serve others and can contribute to whatever newness that people are being pulled together to form.

Marianne Williamson wrote, "As we let our own light shine, we unconsciously give other people permission to do the same." Often when I'm with a group of people, whether on campus as when I was getting my MFA, or at church or some other public forum, someone will comment on how well/content/happy I look and I like to respond by joking, "Yes, but it's my job to look this way." However I'm coming to realize it's not a joke—this really is my job—to create and love and show it is possible to be a certain way in the world.

Now, where do I go from here? Bell said all our own personal stories have existed within us in a "pre-life form" before emerging and manifesting in real life. He asked, "What exists now in you in a pre-life form that hasn't come out yet?" I liked this question. I liked the feel of its forward motion. And here, to my ears, was a way to move toward the answer:

"The more you are you, the more we can be we," he said. The more fearless, joyous, creative you can be, the better it is for everyone. I just have to continue to find those moments, the sweet spots of eternity in which I know I'm reflecting divine light and feeling God's pleasure that I'm doing so.

Earth-shattering? Life-changing? No. But this gives me much needed illumination and affirmation. It does make a difference. Shine a little more light on the road and suddenly I no longer have to putter along in uncertainty. I can see I will keep discerning my own special work. I will pay attention to how it plays into the context of what might be formed with others. I can shift into a higher gear, get off the roundabout, and hit the freeway.

By the way, I think Bell recognized me as a kindred spirit. How do I know? Not because of the warm two-minute exchange we had while I took a picture with him. (He looked at me and said, "Whatever this is you're doing, keep doing it. You have to make sure you keep putting this out in the world.") It was because, as I stood waiting for my friends to get their pictures taken, he turned back to me a couple of times to ask me questions.

He was asking about my name.

With that, Rob Bell and I had come full circle.

OPENING TO LOVE

---

*E*very day my ten-year-old son brings home a vocabulary word we're supposed to discuss over dinner for his homework. They are called "Dinner Plate Words" and after we talk about it he writes out two sentences using the word. Recently his word was "vulnerable." He read a definition out loud: "In a state of weakness; open to attack with lowered defenses." He composed the sentences fairly quickly. One said, "The mouse was vulnerable after the cat attacked it." The other: "The man felt vulnerable after he ran five miles."

I wanted to tell him there is another way to be vulnerable, but I wasn't sure he would understand if I tried to explain the emotional aspect of the word. Maybe I hesitated because I myself am newly confused about it and have much to learn.

Several weeks ago I attended a writers' conference and a panel moderated by a writer whose work I've only just come to know despite the fact that his publishing career spans nearly forty years. We'd met briefly through a mutual friend a few weeks earlier so I would call him an acquaintance. After the session ended I waited until the usual post-talk crowd dissipated. I wanted to say hello and further comment on a question someone else had asked. When it was all clear I approached the writer. He looked at me, then touched his fingers to his lips and held up his hand in greeting. My heart thumped hard, flipping a full somersault in my chest. I paused and checked my steps to make sure I wouldn't fall over. *What in the world was that?* I managed to compose myself and make my comments, but this question has occupied me ever since.

At first I took the easy route: *Oh, I have a crush.* But to use the word "crush"—a silly one, especially at my age—would be to play around quite dishonestly with language. If "crush" were my Dinner Plate Word I'd have to address this definition: "a temporary romantic attraction." This is not romantic and not temporary. On top of this the word sounds wrong, like a childish equivocation. I know I am avoiding something and I am too old not to recognize this feels bigger than a crush—and more important.

This I know for certain. When the elder gentleman touched that kiss my way, he had me. I don't know if he knew it, but he had me. That was it. I loved him from that moment on. I have no idea what he really thinks of me. And I know absolutely nothing about him. He could have a reputation as a notorious flirt for all I know but it really doesn't matter because all I can speak to is what's going on with me. Why did my heart react this way?

There was an awkwardness about him, almost like that of a teenage boy who'd never done this before and was shy and uncertain of how he would be received. This unveiled a vulnerability of his own. His white hair was uncombed, like feathers alighted atop his head and allowed to remain that way to be lifted at will by the slightest air current. His blue eyes, lively behind wireframe glasses, matched his clothing. He dressed in basics as though he'd known for years that if he wore this plain blue blazer with this plain blue shirt he would be assured of looking presentable to the world.

As any flawed human would do, I sifted through useless, common notions (*maybe he reminds me of a grandfather,* or *I'm starstruck by his celebrity*) before I challenged myself to think higher.

The piercing, needle-to-the-heart epiphany came when I finally thought of this: I had been floored by a moment of grace.

What is grace? It is love where it does not have to be, where there is no reason for it. I see grace in acts of affection that occur without explanation—just as the grace God bestows on us every minute of every day. Grace is the love, unconditional and whole, God gives us for no other reason than we are who we are. I think of the John Legend song lyric, "All of me loves all of you/all your curves and all your edges/all your perfect imperfections." I know the singer is thinking romantically, but I always hear God, a God who loves me, in those words. This love carries me through my days. I ride it like a river coursing through my being. It never occurred to me how it could suddenly flow out of me, undammed and free.

I sensed a deep caring pushing me well beyond love. In that moment I stood there and measured my height against this man's and wondered if I could bear his weight if there were ever a time I had to—for instance, turning him onto his side in a hospital bed or lifting him into a wheelchair. He is far from an invalid and yet those thoughts occurred to me. This is not pity—and caregivers already know this—only the deepest love inspires you to the strength required to nurse someone. So this is the best way for me to describe the depth of this immediate love—that I would take care of him.

I can only think my years of exploring God and the human spirit have brought me to this place where my heart is open, quivering and accessible. I am open to love. And now my heart is as exposed and vulnerable as a child without a coat in the rain. Where is my mother mode, my need to cover it up, to protect it? We're supposed to love, love everyone. While this fact usually prompts a discussion of how hard it is to do that, my moment in the conference center made me realize I've come to a point where I have no choice in the matter. My heart loves. It is frightening. It is exhilarating.

I could be making too much of a fleeting moment, but I don't think so. I know I am working on something. I am trying to learn how my heart works. This knowledge, I hope, could be the key to a kind of protection. I would know the landscape of this heart— I would understand its resilience. In this understanding I would gain trust, trust that my heart will survive the slings and arrows that must be visited upon such vulnerability.

This is a dangerous way to be. Even to write this is dangerous because there are so many misconceptions about love. We are quick to categorize—romantic love, filial love, platonic love. We think in terms of marriages, affairs, relationships, and friendships. But I'm only concerned with the love mentioned in Isaiah 43: ". . . *you are precious in my sight, and honored, and I love you*," and the love Christ commanded, that we love one another as we love ourselves. Somehow, I think, we've led ourselves to believe this love is polite and sedentary when in reality it can dash boundaries and crush them to dust. It leaves us exposed—vulnerable.

So this small act, the touch of a kiss and not even a real kiss, has set me whirling with its essence of grace. How can I return it? And not necessarily to this person—I mean can I return it, unconditionally, to everyone I meet? The answer, whether I want it to be or not, must be yes. In one moment love knocked me over with the force of an oceanic wave. I have risen, a total wreck—covered in sand and salt and seaweed. But I recognize I must get up and pursue the living water even as it retreats. I will dive into its heart. I am willing to drown.

OF FLESH AND SPIRIT

here's a scene in Tony Kushner's *Angels in America* when Prior Walter, his body ravaged by AIDS, experiences the vision or hallucination of an angel crashing through his ceiling and descending upon him. His whole being seizes up not in pain, but in a kind of ecstatic spasm. The stage direction in the script reads, "He is washed over by an intense sexual feeling." He later tells a friend he has erections when he perceives the divine visions. When I first saw the scene I remember thinking, yes, that makes sense. That's exactly how it should be. A person so close to the veil would feel the energy tethering him between the earth and his being, and between his being and the divine. And why wouldn't that energy temporarily obliterate his pain and crack him open like a sorcerer's stone through the most sublime release the human body can experience? The angel utters these words: "The body is the garden of the soul."

I like these scenes. I like the shock and exuberance, and the joy of pure physical sensation even in the midst of grave illness. I like the angel's words describing our corporeal beings as the blooming expression of our very essence. I like that Tony Kushner found a way to depict an understanding I've been exploring for a long time concerning this energy, which allows me to confidently be in my body and to respect it and its sexuality. My sense of this energy has led me to this belief: What we do in the privacy of our bedrooms is, in addition to serving procreational and recreational purposes, preparation for something more. It's the practice of an expansion in preparation to be touched from the other side, for a connection to be made complete. Like Michelangelo's Adam reaching out to touch the hand of God, every cell of my being desires my Creator's touch. Sometimes I feel this want to the point where as I walk through the world a breeze can feel like a caress, and a deep breath becomes a life-affirming embrace from within.

I think I've felt this deeper sense, even before I had words for it. Lately I'm beginning to understand this has been, and is, a process. Learning about my body, finding the faith within its very cells, has seemed like a prerequisite to settling into a fine-tuning of antennae, a perfection of a signal so I can recognize the communion when it occurs.

I say "fine-tuning" because if I stray one way or the other, the connection will be lost. Too far in one direction would bring me to a disengaged, puritanical iciness. Too far the other way is the road to lust and its distractions. But somewhere in between these extremes is room for playfulness and a basic enjoyment of the body, this amazing gift and receptor of the world's beauty. So many of us have lost the sense of our natural selves. Or perhaps it wasn't properly fostered when we were children. I remember my mother, or anyone older than me for that matter, would discourage any encounter with "down there." To hear adults tell it, I wasn't supposed to talk about "down there" or, heaven forbid, even touch "down there."

"Get your hands out of your panties, that's nasty."

None of this scolding, though, could discourage my fascination with the smell on my fingers when I pulled them away, or why the scent was strange and familiar all at once. Any further exploration had to be secret, hidden, like I wasn't supposed to know. Because "nasty," as I understood it, described what wasn't supposed to be touched, what wasn't supposed to be done. Oddly enough, this body I wasn't supposed to touch could be praised in other ways. My schoolmates could safely observe I was a fast runner and my coaches that I was strong. My father would say my eyes were so good I could see like an eagle. I was even encouraged to explore these aspects—I could run track, play basketball, throw shot put. Yet the other, the vital aspects of my body, were supposed to be a tremendous secret. A nasty girl, from what I could piece together from what little my parents were willing to say, was someone acting in a realm where she had no business being. Touching yourself a certain way would turn you into such a person. To this day I don't like the word "nasty."

I would be remiss, though, if I didn't acknowledge that my parents had good reason for their warnings—centuries of good reason in fact. I didn't know this then, but being a Black girl automatically put me at a higher risk of sexual abuse. For so long a Black woman's body was simply not her own. Many would argue it's still the case. Today whenever I read an account by a woman of color about rape or incest, often suffered at a young age, I think about how the behavior of my parents that seemed harsh was really protective. They used tactics learned through generations to keep me safe as long as possible. When I was thirteen or so my father had a chain link fence, five feet high, installed, enclosing our house and yard. I used to think it was to keep my four sisters and I in. Now I know it was more a deterrent, to keep danger out. It took me years to understand this fear, and to be grateful for a job well done. No one has messed with my tuning. I am whole and able to feel.

Still, when I hear the word "nasty" in a sexual reference now my heart goes to a place of compassion—first to the person being described, then to the person using the word. Both are struggling, whether they realize it or not, to understand a mystery, a mystery, if left unsolved, leaves them doomed to walk through the world divided because they have left a vital part of themselves in shadow.

I waded through the same confusion. For all its good intentions, the modern day sex education class with its technical definitions of puberty, orgasm, vagina, and such only took me so far. It hid more than it revealed. It didn't explain, for example, the frustrated behavior of a character like Sue Ellen Ewing on the television show *Dallas,* someone who took to drinking because something was dammed up inside her, something that had to do with her husband J. R.'s neglect of her. Even as a pre-teen I could see that.

But I found a glimpse of truth in an Anne Rice novel. I still think of Claudia in *Interview with the Vampire.* Not the version played by Kirsten Dunst in the film but Claudia as originally conceived by Rice—the vampire child who, inwardly, continues to develop with the full-blown needs and desires of a grown woman, but whose desires are forever trapped inside her never-changing child's body. She was my first inkling that what might be called "nasty" was part of a normal, even necessary progression, one tragically stunted in her.

The first time I masturbated to orgasm (how I managed the privacy to do this, I can't remember—my sisters and I slept in two sets of bunk beds in a tiny, tiny bedroom) I didn't understand what I'd done. I thought I'd broken something, especially because I couldn't touch myself again immediately afterward. The spot between the folds of skin was too tender. I turned over onto my side, a little out of breath, and in my mind I heard the thought that still haunts me in moments of enjoyment: *I'm going to get into trouble.* It felt dangerous, like I'd been playing on the edge of a precipice and had fallen over it into a vast abyss. Still, I wanted to walk up to that edge again and again. I'm not sure how long it took before I realized it was okay—I was supposed to jump. The leap was the goal, the reason, the purpose. And—dare I say it?— perhaps the heart of the mystical experience. Just look at Bernini's sculpture depicting the Ecstasy of St. Teresa in a state of spiritual rapture and tell me how it could be otherwise. Describing that ecstatic moment, St. Teresa wrote, "The pain was so severe that it made me utter several moans. The sweetness caused by this intense pain is so extreme that one cannot possibly wish it to cease, nor is one's soul then content with anything but God."

One night, about eight years ago, I had a dream in which I thought God had abandoned me. I was walking through a dilapidated Victorian house with dark wood and many levels—in fact I could see all the floors through to the attic because the ceilings above me had caved in. Rain was coming through and dripping down the walls and fixtures. I had a letter in my hands and I was trying to read it. It was a letter from God. It told me how beloved I am and how he would never be far from me. But I didn't believe it and thought he was already gone because I was surrounded in ruin. Then I had the sensation of a lightning bolt cutting through my body. I opened—no, blossomed—with a force that felt like both sound and sensation prying me open with its echoes. It felt like pure love. I sensed, rather than heard, the words, *How can you doubt me?* The sensation didn't cease. It echoed far and long and upon waking I felt it still.

That morning I took my son to school but afterward I stood in my yard and walked around in circles. I only wanted to feel the warmth of the sun on my body and forever contemplate the love I felt. I wondered if this is why some women enter convents.

Then, more recently, I was stunned to find the exact phrase "I love you" in the Bible. It's in Isaiah 43, "you are precious in my sight and I love you," and I was thrilled to read the words. You could have surrounded me with a thousand Biblical scholars explaining the translation from the original Aramaic and how the prophet is referencing the city of Jerusalem and how the love is metaphorical and I wouldn't listen. Every singing, twitching fiber of my being tells me this verse confirms the letter I dreamed of. This love is for me.

Now everything is about what can bring me closer to that feeling.

I put aside the word "nasty" and walk to this place of inner being, remembering I know how to feel good and what feels good and trust that I am in a realm where not only am I allowed to be, I'm supposed to be. The body is the garden of the soul. Why shouldn't I know it as well as I know where I planted the iris bulbs last autumn in my own yard? I am whole and open. It is a gift to be in this body, to explore the fullness of it, all its possibilities and all of its limitations. To know what it is and what it isn't. It is this knowledge, I am certain, that allows one to shine as a child of God.

Recently I had a massage and while the masseuse worked on me I thought about how people touch each other in general and how it seems a paltry, stingy kind of touching, even in lovemaking, compared to that of a massage. Why aren't we all taught to touch each other like this, at the very least for lovemaking purposes? There's something affirming about the massage touch and it's not just about the pressure. Somehow a massage makes me feel like I really exist. You can talk about our spines and backs (rotate your spine, arch your back, like in yoga classes) all you want, but until someone runs her hand along your vertebrae, only then can you know for certain, "There it is." As she worked her fingers down my back, the knobby chain of bones supporting my frame seemed suddenly real and I wanted to stand up straighter for the knowledge. I felt like clay and with every limb, every muscle, she molded me into being. Only then did I know for certain that the fleshy handful of calf muscle was my leg, and the limbs she pulled over my head like golden ropes were my arms. I kept thinking, *I am here and here and here. I am here.*

But I must be in my body lightly, and hold my physicality gently as I would an apple blossom in my open hand, waiting for it to take flight. Yes, this is my body and it is nothing but dust, but it is important, important enough for God to know He had to take on a body in order to reach us. It is a gift to be in this body, to explore the fullness of it, all its possibilities and all of its limitations. To know what it is and what it isn't. For example, no amount of diet or exercise will trim my calves to the point of fitting them into the tall Frye boots I covet from afar. My legs are simply too thick and muscular. My rear end is a planet all its own. Nearly every pair of pants I own, jeans included, have to be tailored because what fits my legs and butt is too big for my waist. Everything gets taken in. I don't complain about this, though, or wish for something different. I will be in this body now and know it and not complain about it even as it descends into the aches and pains of age.

This summer I found at Walgreen's a $10 tank dress with the same cut and cotton fabric you'd find in a men's sleeveless undershirt. It hangs just above my knees and is the shade of vivid cobalt blue that pulses against the yellow-cake tones of my skin. I could wear it in public but because of its length and form-fitting nature I don't. Not because I would be ashamed or embarrassed. It's because this dress is only for me. I wear it at home during the day when I'm writing. It, like the masseuse, reminds me I have a body. I encounter aspects of myself I might otherwise forget— the childhood scar, a bright star of a keloid, on my right knee; the threads of red and purple veins decorating the tops of my thighs. The color of the dress makes me glow. My body feels sexy and comfortable. I can move. I'm happy I can consider the blushing red spot left on the top of my knee where I have crossed my legs. I'm wondering if more women are beginning to sense the gift of such ease? I'm wondering if that would account for the recent increase in sales of yoga clothing and how it's being used as everyday wear. If so, that gives me hope. And maybe God too.

In the movie Chariots of Fire, the character of the Olympic runner Eric Liddell, as portrayed by Ian Charleson, talks about running being his God-given talent. "God made me fast," he says. "When I run I feel His pleasure." And you can see it too. He begins a race with his torso straight upright, his legs pumping in the disciplined rhythm of a sprinter. But as his speed increases and he leaves his competitors in the dust, a kind of release occurs. His chin lifts, his head thrown backward, and his arms windmill out in sheer ecstasy. When he crosses the finish line you see the faces of people stunned by what they are witnessing. They are no longer watching a race—they are watching him. And watching him with desire and envy and need. He has something they don't even know they want to attain.

Or perhaps they do know. It seems to me the first thing people do when they feel shame and pain is cut off the avenue where God is most likely to reach us—our bodies. We deaden them with drugs, alcohol, cutting, overeating, noise—anything to keep from sensing the grace whispered incessantly—"I love you anyway."

Every six months or so I do a cleansing fast that will last anywhere from five to ten days, but I try to hold out for the whole ten days. The first forty-eight hours are a slog punctuated by skull-chiseling caffeine withdrawal headaches because I'm not drinking my daily two to three cups of strong Irish tea with half-and-half and sugar. If I can make it to day seven or eight, I'm rewarded. That's when a searing clarity blows through me like an April mistral. I see the world in Technicolor. Ideas come swiftly, a blade of grass can bring me joy. My compassion rises easily to the surface and I can walk down the street and feel as though I can hold out my hand and God will simply take it because I can sense He is right there, that close.

It's hard to write these words now because I know the best way to communicate this is to embody it—see by the way I dance. See how I move as though no one is watching—although I very much have a sense of God watching me. I walk around precious in His sight—beloved. Yes, I am all that. But this isn't vanity. Vanity would mean I've put my looks and my body ahead of God and I would be unwilling to let it go, holding it in a desperate, grasping way that could only end in bitterness and frustration. With vanity I wouldn't have the sense of gift or of God enjoying me enjoying my physical presence. I want badly to return the favor.

Once, at a party, a young woman said she admired the free and fearless way I danced.

"It's like you've hacked into this amazing part of your body," she said. "I wish I could do that."

I sipped Coca-Cola, dabbed at my sweaty forehead with a napkin, and considered her compliment. Why would I ever need to hack into some aspect of my body? It's mine. Like a castle with many rooms, or a website with multiple pages, my physical being is a vast expanse of discovery, but I don't need keys or passwords to go where I want it to take me. I have no firewalls in my body.

"I'm not sure I like the word, 'hacked,'" I told her. "It sounds like I'm accessing a place where I'm not supposed to be."

Her eyes widened. She nodded slowly as though remembering something she forgot to tell herself. I wanted to pull her onto the dance floor so we could remember together.

Since the age of ten I've been obsessed with the Franco Zefirelli film *Jesus of Nazareth,* and with the character of Mary Magdalene in particular. She seems to deeply understand the gravity of the physical presence of God in her midst. She touches Him in the humblest of ways, but with the most profound love, by kissing His feet. No one else has touched Christ like this. The elders around Jesus rail at her for defiling Him. But He responds by taking her face in his hands. A relief washes over her like her whole body is sighing. He calls her "Daughter." Even now I weep thinking about it.

Here is my confession. Yes, I go to church and I kneel at the rail and I take in the bread that is Christ's body and the wine that is His blood and I know it all means Communion. But what I really seek, incessantly, perhaps fervently, is a kiss on my forehead and the sensation of His hands on my face and the sound of His voice calling me by my name. Sometimes I think I do feel and hear Him. I have to believe that, even as I prepare to leave this body someday. I have to believe because I know my body will, like Prior Walter's, still vibrate in its reaching out, still craving a soothing completion until it finally shakes itself into dust in its last leap toward the divine. I have to believe an embrace awaits me when I reach the other side.

A FAITH OF PURE IMAGINATION

Alice laughed. "There's no use trying," she said: "one can't believe impossible things."

"I daresay you haven't had much practice," said the Queen. "When I was your age, I always did it for half-an-hour a day. Why, sometimes I've believed as many as six impossible things before breakfast."

—Lewis Carroll, *Through the Looking Glass*

This is how I read Scripture. I'll consume it in small portions, sometimes in a structured setting (at church) and sometimes on my own. There are moments when certain passages, even if I've read them before, will leap off the page and I am inclined to believe the words are naturally speaking to me.

Once I read in Isaiah 43, "You are precious in my sight and I love you," and it felt like a love letter placed in my hands. Of course I am the loved one. Of course I am the precious one. I printed up the words and carried them around for days.

Not everyone, I'm learning, has this comfort level with the Bible. I understand. The text as a whole is daunting and intimidating. So many people, it seems to me, require a well-equipped leader to interpret or provide context before they are willing to delve in. And even then they are like a group of hikers hunkered behind a person tricked out in a headlamp helmet, walking poles, safety gear, and trailblazing tools. I can see how such guidance is useful but I wonder—is it always necessary? Why not take a turn at the front? Why not walk a little on your own?

Recently I discussed this with a friend who also happens to be a seminary graduate. I told him I didn't get why it was so hard to engage with Scripture.

He said, with a smile, "Yes, but not every one has your imagination."

I was stunned. Does faith require imagination? Do I have some sort of "in" because I'm a writer? Is it possible I can more easily accept God's vision of the world because of the worlds I create on paper every day?

As I considered this further certain parts of Scripture took on new meaning. Is this why one must be like a child to enter the Kingdom of Heaven? Who is more expert than a child in the ways of imagination?

When my son was six and attended Sunday school for the first time he was asked to draw a picture of God. I was surprised and fascinated by how he had no trouble doing so. By the way, in case you're wondering, God has big googly eyes, long golden jewelry hanging from large ears, and rows of rings on outstretched fingers. I've kept the picture so I will remember.

If a child can imagine God so easily, then it must work both ways—God has imagined us, after all. We are creatures of divine design. I think the writer Frederick Buechner stumbled upon this concept in an interview when he referred to a "merciful, loving and imaginative God." When the interviewer asks him about the imaginative part, Buechner, who seemed surprised himself, said, "I've never used that phrase before." But he played with it, rolled it around like a bit of clay he'd discovered in his hands. He eventually came up with this: God is "imaginative in the sense that you can't outguess him, you don't know what's going to happen next." Buechner used the Parables as examples, how the stories never turned out how you thought they might. He referred to them as "evidence of the profound and enchanted imagination of Jesus."

I love this vision of godlike play, of imagining helpful stories. But I'm uncomfortable with it in the human sense. What we imagine usually isn't real. But my faith is real. My engagement with Scripture is real. I don't want a faith of pure imagination, a bauble I've crafted myself like a short story or a poem. Such a creation would easily crumble like a sand castle especially, I'm certain, in a time of trouble or tragedy.

Imagination has a dark aspect too. The author Charles Baxter, whose latest collection of short stories, *There's Something I Want You to Do,* is divided into virtues and vices, recently observed in an interview, "In the land of imagination, you think at first that it'll all be peaches and cream. . . . But if you're going to cast your vote for the imagination, you had better be ready for the darkness and craziness, because that's going to be part of the imagination's landscape, too."

He continues: "Having and using the imagination is like living under a spell, and sometimes it's the case that having a good imagination makes your life worse, not better. And the visions you have can come close to killing you. We shouldn't kid ourselves about the imagination's power. It's a fire. It can burn you."

I know something of this because when I was about nine or ten years old I imagined myself into a world that called for me to stop playing outside. I remember the moment precisely. That afternoon my siblings and I were next door, where my father's sister lived, playing "colored eggs" with our cousins. This was a game where one child would be "the fox" who would come to the hen house to ask for colored eggs. The rest of the kids played the eggs and each had secretly chosen a color.

If the fox asked for blue, that "egg" had to run across the yard, touch the gnarly brown telephone pole by the side of the street, and get back to the hen house without being tagged. If the egg got tagged, that person became the fox. I loved this game because I could see it playing out like a movie in my head with all of us rainbow-colored eggs resting in batches of straw in some cozy little chicken coop.

That day, just as I was generating the make believe fox-and-egg world in my mind, another thought intruded. I thought of my father who was in our house asleep in his tattered recliner and the next thing I knew, the movie in my mind changed. In this one I saw him waking up from a post-dinner nap, wondering where everyone was, making his groggy way into the kitchen to find dirty dishes in the sink, the garbage can overflowing, and the clutter that was ever present in our tiny house darkening every corner.

He would get aggravated, then angry, then he would be looking for us, his belt in hand. I remember thinking, "We're going to get into trouble." It snapped me out of my colored eggs daydream.

Even worse, it made me see the game as false and futile, especially since it could only lead to us getting our butts whipped. It was like all the colors had drained away and I saw a stark black-and-white picture that told me the truth of the world. Something in my brain shut off and I couldn't bring myself to the carefree place in my mind where I could play. I walked away from the game—I'm not even sure if anyone noticed—and never went back. The only thing I could do was go inside, do the dishes, and sit and wait for my father to awaken.

As I think back on this now I see how my imagination failed me on two counts: I couldn't imagine the game, but I did imagine getting into trouble, even though it didn't happen. And I continued to live with the expectancy of that dark imagination coming to fruition.

So does this mean imagination is too dangerous, that I should leave it to my fiction and ban it from my spiritual life? Well, no. Imagination does play an important role.

Imagination for me is like a springboard or a launchpad. It provides the required lift to propel myself into faith. But after that initial leap there must be something to grab, something to hold on to. What is that something? I think it's recognizing where God is at work in my life. But even this recognition requires a kind of flexibility.

In this I'm like a trapeze artist reaching out to the guy swinging through the sky to catch me. A few years ago I actually did this at a Club Med in Florida. I climbed three to four stories up the ladder, despite a fear of heights. I swung from the bar and even managed to hook my knees over it so I could swing by my legs and reach out to be caught. But I couldn't execute the maneuver. My back and shoulders weren't flexible enough to bend the way it needed to lengthen my reach and make me catchable.

Perhaps my imagination provides this bit of flexibility faith requires so I can reach across the chasm of disbelief. I can take what might seem like coincidences, or moments of good luck and imagine them as blessings. I can bend farther, make the reach, leap from the bar, and have confidence the Lord will catch me every time.

But you have to look in order to make the grab. Even more so, you have to see, see the love and blessings are real. If I had done this when I was younger I would have focused not on the colored eggs game, but on what was present and real: the feeling of sun on my skin, the joy of being in the company of my siblings and cousins, the lightness of being temporarily free from adult supervision. All this could have upheld me, I think, even if my father had given us all the belt. I might have thought it was worth it.

What do you see? Do you see only a false and futile world full of meaningless coincidences and random twists of fate because a lack of imagination makes it impossible to believe someone could love you so much—so much that he would look after you, bless you, die for you?

And how do you flex your imagination so you can come to believe this impossible thing? As the Queen in *Through the Looking Glass* says, you must practice. You practice with prayer. You practice with listening. Frederick Buechner, in *The Sacred Journey*, wrote "If God speaks to us at all in this world, if God speaks anywhere, it is into our personal lives that he speaks." Practice noticing the impossible, wonderful gifts: when a friend you miss suddenly communicates with you; when help shows up when you need it; when blossoms bloom after a hard winter. Notice and know your faith is real. Then hold on.

HONORING AUTUMN

A DERVISH ESSAY

*H*onoring autumn I turn my face to accept its first golden kiss, one silent plea for attention so honoring autumn I sit on a rock in the forest, patient audience to each leaf tumbling honoring autumn with my presence which autumn returns to me with the word "moment" wrapped in twigs and wild grape vines that fall through my hands so the word disappears at once as I sense it and I offer my full gaze honoring autumn because no one wants to die alone, not even the sugar maple leaves that burn bright red just to make me look and honoring autumn I do and see these leaves aflame and dying as tiny phoenixes again and again and in their smoke I smell cinnamon and in their smoke I smell nutmeg and I receive the promise of their ashes which I need since in honoring autumn I am listening to the bell tolls of my own death gently approaching and I will not miss it as I would if I didn't think to cherish the leaves before a rainstorm knowing many will be loosed before their time and honoring autumn I am hospice preparing flowers for their winter demise and I am hope slipping bulbs like loving secrets into the earth and honoring autumn I remember the seed that sprouted my son planted in me in autumn and how he blooms and blooms an everyday spring reminding me of resurrection even as I am honoring autumn which I must do because death still must come first and I lower my aging body into hot baths so I will not resent the coming cold already creeping over the floorboards and honoring autumn I emerge from this liquid glowing and warm a newborn Venus, baptized and eager to embrace Harvest moon hanging full and heavy like a sleepy baby drunk from his mother's breast and honoring autumn because autumn is orange like my hair and yellow like my skin and brown like my eyes and teaching me how the beauty of all three will soon fall away but autumn whispering hope and autumn whispering love and I am listening autumn and I am once more Red Riding Hood with my basket of light and smiles traipsing through the tangled neverwood of a beloved friend's dream to deliver autumn's message that we are eternal despite the falling all around us and honoring autumn he awakens and remembers he already heard this in a river carrying the autumn leaves away to their watery decay and I awaken to those autumn leaves glowing yellow outside my window and autumn calling me to come for I nearly slept through the moment of their letting go and I rise so I can learn to do the same releasing ego and essence evermore into deep, deep blue autumn skies and what is left of me falls into the softness of the loam returning to the first bed of my being to await the precious breath of the divine drawing me into life again.

CODA

SPEAKING WITH
MY MOTHER NOW

*M*y sister Denise told me she'd had the "end of life" talk with Mom's doctor. This was Thanksgiving 2014 and we stood in Denise's spotless kitchen hours before the cooking began, before the house would fill with our four siblings and their spouses and children. My sister's hands rested palms down on the smooth cool counter and in this gesture I sensed a letting go. She is the best manager of all of my siblings—her house is full of checklists and in her government job she can delegate with a capital "D." But I could tell she had come upon an event she couldn't control. We had thought our mom was still in the early stages of dementia but Denise learned she'd slipped beyond that, quite far. She'd entered the final stage.

The doctor figured Mom had twelve to eighteen months to live but it could be less because her physical condition was poor. The part of her brain that signaled her digestive system was misfiring now and she'd forgotten how to chew and swallow. When I last took care of her in my home, about a year previously, I would serve her a meal and later, sometimes over an hour later, discover she still had small pieces of chicken or soft gobs of collard greens and cornbread in her mouth, often tucked into her cheeks. This is called "pocketing" food and was, though we didn't know it at the time, an early indicator of the final stage. My sister explained someone would have to sit with Mom during Thanksgiving dinner and mimic the chewing action for her or she won't do it. The doctor said Mom eventually would have to go on a liquid diet because her brain won't be able to assemble the right nerve firings to move her jaws, tongue, teeth, and throat in the simple little symphony we mindlessly perform at every meal. At some point the same thing may happen with her respiratory system and her body will forget how to breathe. She has a persistent cough and a throat that won't clear to remind us of this. Everything I'd read about dementia never mentioned physical deterioration. There were plenty of symptom lists mentioning geographic disorientation, short- versus long-term memory loss, and facial recognition. No one talked about how the body can forget it is supposed to be a living, breathing, being.

That evening, after our Thanksgiving dinner, Denise placed Mom's wheelchair by a window in the front of the house so Mom could watch her putting Christmas lights on the bushes outside. Everyone else was in the family room or kitchen watching football and eating pie. I pulled over a chair and sat next to her and it felt very much like the times I would sit with my father on my visits home when I was in my early twenties and realized the best gift I could offer him was my presence. Only I knew no monologues would erupt from my mother—nothing requiring a response. No "Yes, ma'am's" for her that would add up to the multitudes of "Yes, sir's" for him. Instead she sat like an obedient child, patiently waiting. I couldn't tell if she had any interest in the bright spots of blue, yellow, red, and green levitating from my sister's hands outside the window.

Finally I asked, "Are you enjoying your Thanksgiving, Mom?"

She nodded but I could tell by the thin line of her lips and the way she pushed her glasses back up on her nose that something was on her mind, something she was trying to figure out.

"I don't know if we had dinner yet, though," she said.

"We did, Mom," I said. I didn't want her to worry so I modeled an image of unconcern as best I could. I sat back in my seat, crossed my legs, and looked out the window. "But it's okay," I continued. "If you get hungry later you can eat something else. There's plenty of pie in there still."

She nodded. We sat in silence again.

For a brief time I prayed with my mother every day. At 5:30 p.m. the preset alarm on my iPhone would sound with a tickling chime called "Illuminate." I would dial her number from wherever I was, usually at home, but on various Tuesdays or Thursdays I'd be at church waiting for my son to finish choir rehearsal. She'd answer and ask, "Are you ready?"

"Yes, Mom."

Sometimes we'd recite the Lord's Prayer together. Sometimes she'd say one of the countless prayers, Psalms, or religious poems she knew by heart. I learned to have *The Book of Common Prayer* close by in case she said, "Your turn now," and I'd have to come up with something. Of course it would have made sense for me to have a prayer at the ready, but I admit I easily leaned on her expertise. This was partly because she was more powerful at the prayer business. But really it was about my hearing her voice, and having the sound of her lay over my being like the hand of Isaac delivering a blessing. And I admit I needed this feeling, needed it so I would stop not returning her phone messages, so I could recover the sense of honoring her as my mother.

I got the idea for these prayer dates during a week when I was taking care of Mom not long after my sister Theo died and my siblings and I had moved Mom to the D.C. area where two of my sisters lived and could better care for her. Back then she lived in an apartment down the hall from Denise. The first afternoon I was there Mom and I were sitting in the living room with the Game Show channel on, which she watches in perpetuity except when it's time for "Bonanza" reruns. Mom was crocheting—she could still grasp the hooked needle and yarn despite the

swelling in her finger joints. On the table next to her the phone
rang and she picked it up with the attitude of a woman going to
work or, more exactly, a child imitating an adult in an office. She
exchanged brief pleasantries while I turned the volume down on
Match Game and its host, Gene Rayburn. Mom's voice took on
the cadence of reciting verse and I realized she was saying something about Jesus's love. After a few more niceties she hung up
and went back to crocheting.

"Who was that, Mom?" I knew she hadn't been in the area
long enough to make any local acquaintances, surely none that
would already call.

"A woman I know from my church back home. She calls me
every day and we pray together."

I nodded and turned back to the jokes of Nipsey Russell and
the Technicolor outfits, as bright as they were in my childhood,
of Charles Nelson Reilly. But I felt a pull inside of me I can only
describe as three strands of thought about Mom's practice of
praying with this woman:

> *I could do that*
> *I should do that*
> *I don't want to do that*

It took about two years of these thoughts twisting about in
my head to form a braid strong enough to say, *I want to do that.*
This braid I pulled. This braid drew me to my mother.

It took two years because other understandings had to come
first and I was slow in the learning. I had to figure out that avoid-
ance, like not answering phone messages, never solves the issue
when I have a problem with someone. Instead of running away
from the person I have to run toward them, immerse myself in
them, allow him or her to set up residence in my heart instead of
my head and court them with a measure of my thoughts. A good
way to do this is for me to pray for the person, saying his or her
name out loud in my personal prayers during the week and at
the Prayers of the People in church on Sundays. Once I spent an
entire Lenten season praying daily for a writer who'd not been

kind in our social interactions. After forty days of praying for an acquaintance I realized I owed my mother—and myself—the same attention, and the chance to claim an area of my being already her own.

Our practice didn't last long—perhaps longer than forty days but less than a year. I realized the unexpected benefit of no more unreturned phone messages because as long as I called at our appointed time daily Mom never had to initiate calls or leave messages. Some days I dialed easily and the prayer was swift and light. Some days the alarm would go off and I would sit staring at the phone for a while but I would call, eventually. I did let her know if I couldn't call at all—if I would be traveling for instance. Over time Mom had to move into assisted living and then into a nursing home. She wore a cell phone on a lanyard around her neck but as time went on she couldn't remember to charge it. Then she couldn't remember how to answer or dial the phone and it was my turn to leave messages that went unanswered. I stopped calling.

⁂

I don't know why, but sitting with my mother that Thanksgiving evening, I thought of our phone calls and realized we could talk to each other, that we had a common language, a way of speaking that was hardwired into her cells. Many people with dementia will recall song lyrics or sports statistics or dance steps because their bodies remember even if their minds can't clearly think why. I knew my mother would remember how to pray.

"Mom," I said, "it's time for Evening Prayer. Do you want to do it with me?"

She nodded and I retrieved my Kindle from my bag and opened the Daily Office. I read through it, pausing so she could repeat what I'd recited in a call and response way. When I saw that she was intent on repeating everything I said, I skipped the lengthier Scripture readings and kept to the shorter bits—the collects, selections from Isaiah, the Magnificat, and the Apostles Creed. Finally we recited the Lord's Prayer. When we finished she looked at me.

"Do you have any more of them prayers?"

My mouth fell open. A tingling wave of shock and surprise swept through me. I was so happy something had engaged her I would have gotten her plane tickets to Paris if she had asked for them. "Yes!" I replied. I opened the Kindle again and my fingers flew over the screen. In addition to a year's worth of the Daily Office, I also have the Bible and St. Augustine's Prayer Book on my tablet so I quickly found something else for us to pray. At some point as I was leaning toward her so she could hear me, she must have realized she could see the large print words on my Kindle and, surprising me once more, she started reading along with me in unison. My sister-in-law captured the last few minutes of this on video. In the clip I'm wearing a black turtleneck sweater and I have reading glasses perched on my nose. Mom's hands are folded in her lap and there's a small dot of light near her right eye, the glowing screen of the Kindle reflected in her glasses. I'm pointing out the words to her line by line and prompting her when she stumbles over words. When we get to the final line of "A Collect for Fridays" she struggles a bit more and I can tell she's tired. *Mercifully grant that we, walking in the way of the cross, may find it none other than the way of life and peace; through Jesus Christ your Son our Lord. Amen.*

"That's enough of that for tonight," she said. She glanced at my sister-in-law's camera phone, a small smile on her lips.

"That was great, Mom," I said. I took off my glasses. "Oh my goodness."

❧

It's been sixteen months since that Thanksgiving and my mother, now eighty-four, is still with us. She lives in a steady state of now. Sometimes she is forty-five in her now. Sometimes she is eighty-two and marveling over how much Tain has grown. He knows not to say anything when she asks repeatedly how old he is and what grade he's in. He answers with patience every single time, reminding me, as he always does, to grasp love in both hands and jump.

One day, sitting in her wheelchair in her room in the nursing home, she announced to me, "Sophfronia, I'm dying."

Her voice, however, didn't sound like the voice of a dying woman. It was strong and clear—clearer than I'd heard it in ages because of her persistent, phlegmy cough. I sat on the side of the bed, leaned toward her and looked into her face. She didn't seem distressed or sad but I saw, as I often do, the same cloudy look of concern, like there's something she had to do but couldn't quite remember what.

"How do you know, Mom?"

She shrugged and tugged at the little blue turban she likes to wear over her thinning hair when she's not wearing a wig. "I just know. I feel like I'm running down. I don't know how to let go, though."

For years I have spoken to my mother in the same tones I would use to humor a child. She never seemed to want more from me, even before the dementia—I always felt she stopped listening if I went deeper into anything beyond the news, the weather, or Tain's school activities. But in that moment, perhaps for the first time ever, I spoke to my mother as I would another adult.

"It's going to be okay," I said. I spoke slowly and enunciated carefully. I want her to know her brilliance in this particular area. I want to remind her of her power. "You already know this, you know it better than anyone. When the time comes you'll know what to do and you won't be alone."

Tain once asked me, "Could Grandma Ruby ever forget God?" I told him no, that even if she didn't have the words; she would have the feeling. I looked into my mother's eyes and hoped my words would trigger that feeling, if that was indeed what she needed. She rubbed her hands together and nodded.

A nursing home aide brought in the tray and plastic dishes containing Mom's dinner. Mom gestured at the food. "God is great," she said. "God is good. Let us thank him for our food. Amen."

I pulled the rolling table closer to her chair and sighed. "Amen."

❦

Sometimes when I speak with my mother now I am a grown woman and sometimes I am, to her, four years old and in need of my bath before bedtime. One night she tells me she didn't know if my brother Wayne had clean clothes for school the next day. She says she must comb and braid my and my sisters' hair. My heart softens for this young woman puzzling over how to juggle the needs of her brood of small children. I sense the authentic love I was probably too stubborn to notice or admit by the time I hit my tweens. I too return to those early years so I can remember. Back then I shared a bed with two of my sisters and I recall the feel of Theodora's five-year-old hands in my hair, undoing the thick braids our mother had carefully plaited the night before. Asleep, she would suck her thumb with one hand and with the other play with my hair. I complain about this to my mother now as we sit in her nursing home room and I lobby, as I once did, to sleep on the other side of the bed with my sister Denise between me and Theo.

Denise prays Mom doesn't suffer but I don't believe she will. For myself I'm not so sure. I have no idea what it will be like for me when my mother passes. I don't know if all my praying and presence will be enough for me to let her go, or if her death will make some void harsh and apparent—something I should have said, something I didn't do. Is the cloud of worry on her face a mirror of what mine will become?

My mother is walking through the vesper light. I join her as I can but I know she will soon outpace me. It is an intriguing path we walk, she and I. I have no doubt it is paved in forgiveness.

21ST CENTURY ESSAYS
David Lazar and Patrick Madden, Series Editors

This series from Mad Creek Books is a vehicle to discover, publish, and promote some of the most daring, ingenious, and artistic nonfiction. This is the first and only major series that announces its focus on the essay—a genre whose plasticity, timelessness, popularity, and centrality to nonfiction writing make it especially important in the field of nonfiction literature. In addition to publishing the most interesting and innovative books of essays by American writers, the series publishes extraordinary international essayists and reprint works by neglected or forgotten essayists, voices that deserve to be heard, revived, and reprised. The series is a major addition to the possibilities of contemporary literary nonfiction, focusing on that central, frequently chimerical, and invariably supple form: The Essay.